IMAGES
of America

ISSAQUAH
WASHINGTON

This view of the Issaquah Valley, taken in 1943 from Squak Mountain, shows the landscape before the development boom of the 1960s. (94.21.15)

IMAGES
of America

ISSAQUAH
WASHINGTON

Issaquah Historical Society

ARCADIA
PUBLISHING

Published by Arcadia Publishing
Charleston, South Carolina

Library of Congress Catalog Card Number: 2002109310

For all general information contact Arcadia Publishing at:
Telephone 843-853-2070
Fax 843-853-0044
E-mail sales@arcadiapublishing.com
For customer service and orders:
Toll-Free 1-888-313-2665

Visit us on the Internet at www.arcadiapublishing.com

A wave of laborers, like these 1908 Grand Ridge Mine crew members and High Point Mill crew members came to the Issaquah area in the early 1900s. (93.32.1.50)

CONTENTS

ACKNOWLEDGMENTS

We are indebted to community members who placed photographs in our care over the years. Because of them, we have a varied collection with which to tell Issaquah's story. Thanks also go to participants in the 2001 Memory Book Project, whose writings are frequently quoted in this volume.

Museum Director Erica S. Maniez wrote text and coordinated project details, with help from Administrative Assistant Lisa Clapper. However, like most of our organization's accomplishments, this one would not have been possible without volunteers. *Images of America: Issaquah, Washington* would not have met its deadline without the dedication of Diane Dambacher. Christina Asavareungchai, Jean Cerar, Penny Miller, and Leslie Schuyler also contributed greatly to the production of this volume. David Bangs, Jean Cerar, Eric Erickson, Faye Green, Linda Adair Hjelm, and Nancy Horrocks provided project oversight.

Warm thanks go to David Bangs for donating many of the contemporary images, and to Greg Spranger for providing depot restoration photographs. Finally, we wish to acknowledge Moon Photo in Seattle for its high-quality photograph reproduction services.

Boxed goods are stacked on the wooden sidewalk of Mill Street (today's Sunset Way) in this winter scene from the 1930s. The Rolling Log Tavern, Grand Central Hotel, and Snoqualmie Power Station are also visible. (72.21.14.128)

6

INTRODUCTION

In many ways, the history of Issaquah is typical of the region east of Seattle and Lake Washington. Like so many other towns in the area, its early history bears the marks of the railroad, mining, and logging. However, other elements make the town's history unique. Issaquah is one of the oldest settlements east of Lake Washington and its story includes King County's first hop farms, the recall of the town's first female mayor, and the organization of Salmon Days, one of the most popular regional celebrations in the country. And although growth and development has changed the face of the town, many elements of its original character remain.

In creating this book, we set out to include photographs that not only document the history of Issaquah, but which also capture the spirit of the town in all its phases of development. We drew from historic images in our collection, but have also included a number of contemporary images in order to document Issaquah's more recent past. We hope that this volume will appeal to residents who have lived here all their lives, and bring back memories of days gone by. We also think that those who have come to the area recently will recognize the Issaquah they know in these pages, and develop an appreciation for the history of their new hometown.

The process of creating this book included an extensive inventory of our photograph collection. It also included a series of photograph identification days, where long-time residents of the area sat down with us and shared their memories of the events depicted. We tried to look at our collection with fresh eyes; as a result many of the images selected for this book have never before been published.

The Issaquah Historical Society cares for a collection of more than 2,000 historic images. This is a small fraction of the historic education work we undertake. The Issaquah Historical Society was formed in 1972 by a group of Issaquah residents who felt that the preservation of the community's rich history—in architecture, photographs, artifacts, and stories—was vital to its future. Today, the Issaquah Historical Society operates two museums, the Gilman Town Hall and the Issaquah Depot, as well as a restoration center, in historic buildings. It offers group tours, research services, and a variety of educational programs. You can learn more about the Issaquah Historical Society and its work at our website, www.issaquahhistory.org. If you are interested in obtaining copies of any of the images in this book, please contact us at 425-392-3500 or info@ issaquahhistory.org.

Town of Issaquah

The south end of Squak Valley was raw and stump-filled in 1890, but residences and business buildings were starting to fill it when this picture was taken. (95.14.1)

One

BECOMING A
BOOM TOWN
1860–1920

The first white settlers came to the area now called Issaquah in the 1860s, scarcely ten years after the Denny Party landed at Alki Point. They named the area Squak, a corruption of the Native American place name "isquowh," which means "sound of water birds." These early settlers were drawn to the area by fertile farmland. Issaquah's earliest commercial crop was hops, which was introduced in 1868. By the 1890s a number of families in the valley were planting and harvesting hops. Although coal was discovered in 1862, deposits in the area were not immediately mined. Without a quick way to transport the coal to market, a major coal industry was cost-prohibitive. The town seemed destined to remain a quiet farming community.

But in the late 1880s, the Squak Valley settlement was suddenly transformed into a thriving town. The Seattle Lake Shore & Eastern Railroad reached the valley in 1887, and the depot was completed two years later. With fast transport to Seattle now available, mining promised to become a profitable venture. The development of area coal seams began in earnest. The quickly growing town incorporated as Gilman in 1892, becoming the first incorporated town on the east side of Lake Washington. In 1899 the residents voted to change its name, and thus Issaquah was born.

The blossoming coal industry brought an influx of workers, many of them immigrants, seeking employment in the mines. The logging industry also flourished during this time, and more workers arrived to fell trees and establish sawmills. The industry brought not only laborers to town, but also merchants looking for a market. By 1910 Issaquah boasted a creamery, bank, newspaper, insurance agency, hardware store, meat market, and clothier.

In this early, rough-cut Issaquah, the only business establishments that outnumbered hotels were saloons. On weekends the jail could fill quickly as the tough workingmen spent their wages on whiskey. For the laborers who came to the valley to work, life could be brutal. Working in the mines and mills was difficult and often dangerous work. But for men like the Tibbetts brothers, W.W. Sylvester, William E. Gibson, and others, Issaquah offered opportunities for success.

The first residents of Squak Valley were the Sammamish Indians. The Sammamish were a band of the Duwamish tribe, and they had regular camps on the shores of the lake that today bears their name. Like many other tribes in the Puget Sound region, they spoke Lushootseed, or the Coast Salish language. Just to the east of the Sammamish lived the Snoqualmie. Pictured here is Mary Louie, a medicine woman of the Snoqualmie tribe, who lived in Squak Valley and knew many of the early white settlers. (86.18.303)

This family of Native Americans lived along the shores of Lake Sammamish c. 1890–1900. Note that they have adopted European-style dress. Pictured from left to right are unidentified, Elsie Zackuse Erickson, Cora Zackuse Ramirez, and Tom Zackuse. (86.18.306)

In 1868 the Wold brothers planted half an acre of hops, purchased from Ezra Meeker. By the 1890s, many white settlers in Squak Valley were growing hops. They employed both Native American and white workers to pick the crops. An attempt at hiring Chinese laborers in 1885 resulted in violence. White and Native American pickers, fearing a loss in wages, killed four Chinese pickers and drove the rest out of town. (91.36.2)

These Native American hops pickers are migrant workers from east of the Cascade Mountains and worked in the Wold hop fields in the 1880s. Native Americans in the Puget Sound area did not use tepees. The Wold brothers (Lars, Ingebright, and Peter) were among the earliest white settlers in the area. (93.32.1.24)

At the end of the season, hops were dried in massive hop kilns before they were sold to breweries in Seattle. These kilns were on the Wold farm. (93.32.1.14)

Some of Issaquah's earliest settlers were Civil War veterans. Shown here, c. 1900, are local members of the Grand Army of the Republic, a Union veterans' organization, and three of the gentlemen's granddaughters. Pictured from left to right are: (front row) unidentified, James Stevenson, William Brunk, unidentified, William S. Gibson, and Olive (Gibson) Bayh; (back row) unidentified, John Berry, Alice Giese, (?) Prillman, George W. Tibbetts, Cora Bea (Goode) Lassen, Sylvanus Baxter, and James Forsman. (72.21.14.130)

George W. Tibbetts was one of Issaquah's earliest entrepreneurs. In addition to his hotel and store (pictured above), he also became involved in farming hops and running a stage line, as well as in local and state government. The hotel shown here was built in 1884 and burned to the ground in July 1900. (92.24.6)

13

James and Martha Bush arrived in Seattle in 1859, and moved to Squak Valley in the early 1860s when the city became too crowded for their liking. The Bushes were among the first white residents in the valley. (2002.16.1)

Lyman B. Andrews discovered coal deposits in Squak Valley in 1862. Shortly thereafter, he purchased a claim and came to the area with his family to live. The claim proved unprofitable at that time, due to the cost of transporting the coal to Seattle. This realization, along with an injury, influenced the Andrews family's move back to Seattle in 1865. (92.29.2)

Farming continued to be the main source of revenue among valley residents until the 1890s. In this 1895 photograph, Mount Rainier is visible from Lawrence and Floss Smart's farm, located near the shores of Lake Sammamish. The Pickering barn is visible in the background. (2001.33.2)

From 1893 until 1904, Wilhelm and Sophia Goebel and their children had a farm northwest of Issaquah, near Pine Lake. Pictured from left to right are members of the Goebel family: John, Rosalie, Mary, Agnes, Sophia, Wilhelm, William, and Frederick Goebel. (94.19.1)

As the number of settlers grew, so did the need for a school. One of the earliest schools in Squak Valley was operated on Pickering's Hill, overlooking the valley. Pictured from left to right, c. 1890, are: (on ground) Ernest Pickering, (?) Prigmore, and Ed Tibbetts; (standing, front) Roy Pickering, Herman Settem, William Pickering III, Bessie (Wilson) Craine, Annie Jackson, Maude Shaw, Ralph Darst, Jeannette Thompson, unidentified, Katie McCluskey, unidentified, Jake Jones, Inez Darst, and Del Wold; (back row) teacher J.H. Kirkpatrick, unidentified, Tom McCluskey, Ida Mae (Tibbetts) Goode, Bertha Baxter, Charles Shaw, unidentified, and Wilson Tibbetts. (86.104.1)

16

In 1887 the Seattle Lake Shore & Eastern Railroad (SLS&E) reached Squak Valley, and in 1889 the depot was completed. The railroad transformed the sleepy farming valley into a center of commerce, and inspired townspeople to name their home after Daniel Hunt Gilman, one of the SLS&E's owners. This photograph was taken on August 14, 1892, after the town's incorporation as Gilman. (86.87.18)

In 1899 a formal petition from Gilman's town council requested the Washington State Legislature to designate Issaquah the town's new name. Behind the Issaquah Depot, the false front of the Davis Hotel is visible. The Davis was one of many hotels in Issaquah c. 1900. (89.13.34A)

The railroad gave citizens in Gilman a way to transport goods into Seattle quickly. Coal became a profitable business, and a number of mines were established in the early 1890s. As the coal industry boomed, other merchants came to the town to establish businesses of their own. The bridge over Issaquah Creek shown in this 1889 photograph was the only means of reaching the mine and corresponding company homes. (72.21.14.180)

Workers from all over, many of them immigrants, flooded into the area to work the mines, and the population of the town swelled. These miners were employed by the Pacific Coal Company, c. 1920. Erick Erickson Sr. is pictured here (second from the right), and the others are unidentified. (86.18.266B)

Rail spurs led from the depot to the mines. In this manner, coal could be easily transported to the depot, and then on to Seattle. Note the rails and coal cars evident in this photograph. Pictured from left to right are Joe Favini, Joe Yourglich, George Thomas, unidentified, unidentified, and George Pedro. (72.21.14.186A)

Alvo von Albensleben, a German citizen backed by German investors, owned the Issaquah and Superior Coal Mine. The mine, part of the claim originally discovered by Andrews, was said to be capable of producing more than 2,000 tons of coal daily. In 1913, the year of this photograph, the company built more homes and business buildings than it had built in the preceding 20 years. However, Albensleben's financial support dried up when World War I started in 1914. (86.18.222A)

Other mines in the Issaquah area included the Grand Ridge, Bianco, Harris, and Caroline mines. Pictured here are ten unidentified miners standing in front of the Grand Ridge mine. The Grand Ridge ceased operations in 1920. (86.18.221B)

Many miners lived in company homes constructed by the coal company. The area where they lived was called Mine Hill. Some of the original homes still stand on Mine Hill Road and Wildwood Boulevard. (2001.39.3)

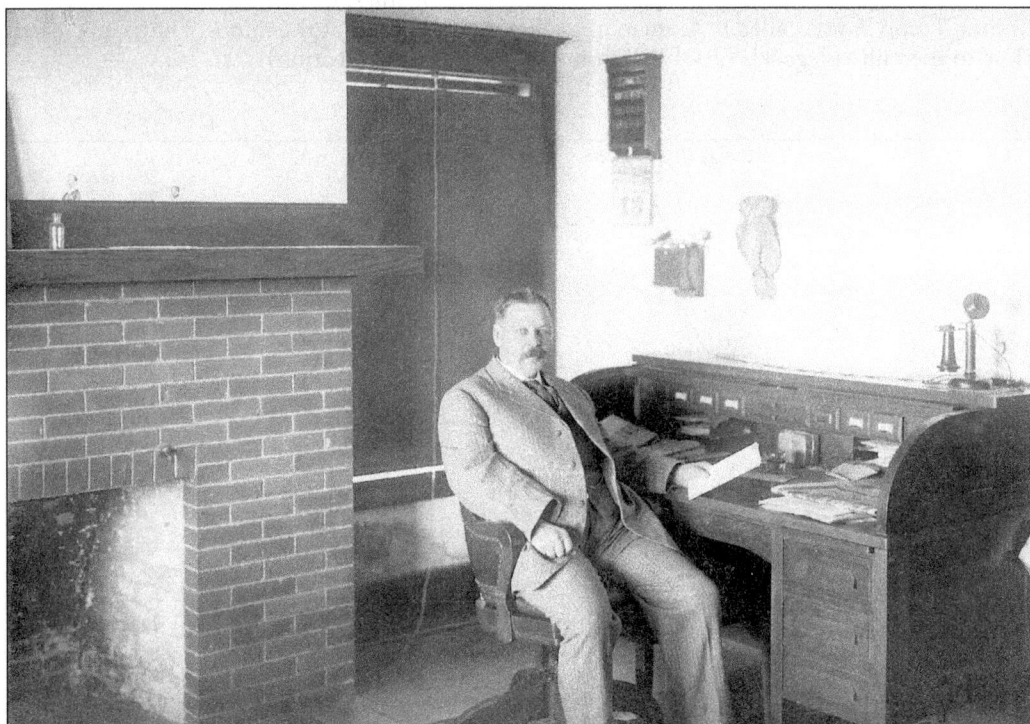

Dr. Hiram R. Corson came to Issaquah to work for the Issaquah Coal Company in the role of company doctor from 1900 to 1910. He also served as the mayor of Issaquah from 1903–1908. (72.21.14.176)

Labor unrest was a recurring problem for the mining companies. In 1891, the Washington State Militia, Troop B, was called to Gilman to quell potential unrest at the mines. They set up camp close to the railroad tracks. (2001.9.1, from the Jeff Dygert Collection)

This photograph of the 1891 militia encampment also offers a view of the Davis Hotel, with Squak Mountain in the background. (2001.9.5, from the Jeff Dygert Collection)

Seattle Lake Shore & Eastern Railway car #574 was in the background as Troop B relaxed. Although this scene looks candid, photography methods of the time required subjects to hold a pose. Several subjects in this photograph moved, creating blurs. (2001.9.6, from the Jeff Dygert Collection)

Troops prepare to break camp and leave Gilman. Unrest and strikes continued until the 1920s. By the time the golden age of coal was drawing to a close, trade unions and mine superintendents were in constant and often violent conflict. Labor troubles and economic decline both contributed to the closing of many Issaquah mines. (2001.9.3, from the Jeff Dygert Collection)

The lumber industry also attracted newcomers to Issaquah. At one time the hills surrounding the Issaquah valley were clear-cut to provide lumber for the Seattle market, and for local construction. Pictured from left to right are Alfred Kerola and John Barlow, wielding a two-man saw on one of the area's giant cedar trees. Each man stands on a springboard set into the tree. (95.16.1)

This photograph shows the impressive size of the old-growth lumber logged in the area. (86.18.242E)

Hundreds of sawmills and lumber operations have existed in Issaquah over the years. The first sawmill was the Donnelly Mill, established at Lake Sammamish's south end in the 1870s. This photograph of Vaughan's Mill employees was taken c. 1900. Several individuals in the back row are identified: Hattee (Hamilton) Vaughan (third from left), Myrtle (Bush) Horrocks (sixth from left), Dave Horrocks Sr. (seventh from left), and Floyd Bush (seated child, far right). (2002.1.22)

The Neukirchen family founded the Neukirchen Mill in 1910, the year this photograph was taken. Their planing mill was located just south of downtown, and west of the intersection of today's Front Street and Second Avenue, while the sawmill was located four miles south of Issaquah. The Neukirchen Mill operated until 1918. (2001.27.1)

Steam donkeys were widely used in logging operations, and common elements in logging photographs of the era. Steam donkeys were used to pull logs from the forest to a central point. They were called steam donkeys because they were steam powered, and their engines were smaller than one horsepower. Steam donkeys did the work previously done by horses and bulls. The logging operation pictured here was in Preston. (92.28.10)

Like the coal mines, Issaquah's lumber mills and logging operations had their own rail spurs that allowed them to move lumber to the Seattle market. In this photograph, c. 1910–1920, an Allen and Nelson mill employee climbs aboard a car bound for the Pine Lake Plateau logging operations. (2001.21.1)

The timber industry also gave rise to new communities in outlying areas. In 1906, High Point was a mill town of 40 shingle mill employees and their families. Identified employees of the High Point Mill Company, pictured from left to right, are: (front row) Pete Erickson, Erick Erickson Sr., unidentified, unidentified, unidentified, and Hugo Johnson; (back row) Erick Erickson Jr. (far left), and David Horrocks Sr. (fourth from left). (74.52.2B)

The lumber town of Monohon was located a few miles north of Issaquah on the banks of Lake Sammamish. The Allen and Nelson Mill Company began operations in Monohon in 1889. This was excellent timing in some ways. Seattle's Great Fire occurred in the same year, and rebuilding efforts required a great deal of lumber. The setting of this photograph is the Pine Lake Plateau east of Monohon. Pictured here are typical logging practices and equipment of the era. (86.18.229)

28

This photograph of Monohon shows the mill and the company homes constructed around it. In addition, Monohon contained a post office, community store, hotel, and school. The town also boasted a literary club, and a chapter of the Modern Woodsmen. (91.7.14)

In 1925 the Bratnober Lumber Company (previously Allen and Nelson) fell prey to a fire. The company store, pictured here in 1909, was destroyed, as were the hotel, post office, railroad depot, and 50 company homes. Only a handful of the company homes were spared. Although the mill was eventually rebuilt, the community of Monohon ceased to exist. (91.7.13)

Preston, six miles east of Issaquah, was another town created by the lumber industry. The Preston Mill Company was founded in 1892 by Emil Lovegren, a Swede, and six other Scandinavians. The mill produced only shingles until 1900, when a sawmill was added at Upper Preston, expanding production. (94.1.9)

The Upper Preston sawmill was constructed on the banks of the Raging River. A two-mile flume was built from the Upper Preston sawmill to the Preston mills. Rough lumber was sent down the flume for final processing before being shipped by rail. This photograph, c. 1910, gives a rare view of the millpond where logs were stored before being sent down the flume. Notice the Climax engine coming towards the mill from the left. (94.1.4)

Like most mill towns, Preston had its own post office and general store, shown here. As of 1913, Preston also had a hotel, YMCA hall, basketball court, and heated "plunge," or swimming pool. (94.1.2)

Preston residents assemble in front of the cookhouse. When this photograph was taken in 1923, the Preston mill was still going strong. It continued operating until 1992. (92.28.12)

While the mines and mills generated income and brought workers to town, other businesses flourished by providing lodging and drink. Hotels and saloons were numerous in early Issaquah. The Bellevue Hotel, pictured here *c.* 1912, was located on the southeast corner of what is today Front Street and Sunset Way. Pictured from left to right are Jarred Trigg, Chuckie Robinson, Dan Loftus, and Lorenzo Francis. (87.144.28)

Mary and Thomas Francis built the Bellevue Hotel, a large establishment for its time, in 1888. After Thomas's death in 1899, Mary continued to operate the hotel by herself. Gathered on the hotel's porch, from left to right, are Chuckie Robinson, Jarred Trigg, Mary (Cartwright) Francis, Lorenzo Francis, and Dan Loftus. Two of the canine friends have been identified as Punch (in chair) and Guess (held by Mrs. Francis). (87.144.21)

James Croston built the Grand Central Hotel in 1903. The Croston family operated the hotel until 1920. Since then it has had many owners. It is the last remaining hotel from Issaquah's boomtown era. Sadly, years of neglect have made it difficult to recognize it as the same building in this 1924 photograph. (95.23.1)

Town Marshall Howard Case (left) stands in front of Clark's Saloon with proprietor George Clark. This photograph was taken in 1912. Evidently there had been some altercation shortly before the photograph was taken. The right window was broken and replaced, but the saloon's name had not yet been repainted on the pane. (91.7.1)

The Klondike Bar, owned by Burn Mallarkey, was another saloon on Front Street. In this photograph, the bar has been decorated for Christmas. (73.9.158)

A group of men stands in front of the Pastime, another Front Street saloon offering the additional enticement of pool and billiards. Next door is the Palace of Sweets, operated by Annie Favini, Edith McQuade, and Ethel McQuade. (89.40.1)

Since no citizen could survive on saloons alone, other businessmen could be certain of making a profit in this booming town. John W. Finney founded his meat market in 1904, and moved into this building in 1910, after a fire destroyed the original building. Finney's Meats later competed with Fischer's Market, founded in 1913. Fischer's, located on Front Street, is still in business today. (89.10.4)

W.M. Clark's blacksmith shop was located on Front Street next to the IXL Livery. (89.13.30C)

J.J. Lewis founded Lewis Hardware Store in 1903. In this 1920 photograph, his son Tom is minding the store. Lewis Hardware has provided necessities for several generations of Issaquah residents, and is still in operation today. Colleen Darst Petersen remembers, "You could get just about anything you needed and they would tell you how it worked at the same time. It was always like going home." (92.16.1)

E.J. Anderson's store, founded in 1909, offered hardware, feed, and building supplies. The store was located on the northeast corner of today's Front Street and Sunset Way. When Anderson retired in 1924, he sold the store to Andy Wold. Pictured from left to right are Joe Pedegana, Tom (?), Art Liebich, Ed "Nogs" Seil, (?) Humes, (?) Humes, Jess Walker, and E.J. Anderson. (92.1.1)

Andy Wold, son of hop farmer Lars Wold, operated A.L. Wold Hardware Store. The store was located on the corner of today's Front Street and Sunset Way. In this 1924 photograph are, from left to right, Walford Isotalo and Charlie Smith. (85.9.155)

Henry Kinnune learned the cobbler's trade from his father. He also inherited his father's shoe repair shop in Issaquah. (72.21.14.213)

Wilbur W. Sylvester founded the Bank of Issaquah in a modest clapboard building in 1900. In 1910, Sylvester held a grand opening at this imposing new building on Front Street. The building still stands on the northwest corner of today's Front Street and Alder Street. This photograph was taken c. 1914–1916. (72.21.14.179A)

The interior of the Bank of Issaquah was rich with detail. Note the art deco trim along the ceiling. The building was known as one of the most sophisticated in Issaquah. Its current appearance is due to a renovation in the 1940s, which covered up its ornate detailing. By the time this picture was taken in 1914, the bank had changed hands and had become the Issaquah State Bank. (78.59.4)

Victoria Ek was employed by Sylvester for many years. She worked at the bank, and also served as Issaquah's treasurer in 1914. This unconventional working woman is seen here on a camping trip with her sisters. Pictured here, from left to right, are Sam Mercer, Esther (Ek) Peterson, Mabel (Ek) Brady, Victoria Ek, Dessie (Green) Mercer, and infant (?) Mercer. (72.21.14.91 B)

Growth in Issaquah's population required a larger schoolhouse. Although the students are numerous in this photograph, c. 1900, the town would not hold a high school graduation ceremony until 1911. Classes were held only through eighth grade. In this era, many young people went to work in the fields, mines, or homes before they could earn a diploma. (85.18.1)

By 1905, the size of the town's school had doubled. The building depicted in the previous photograph forms a wing of this building. This photograph was taken c. 1910. (91.5.18)

In 1911 the first graduates from Issaquah High School were, from left to right, Mary Gibson, Olive (Gibson) Bayh, and Mabel (Ek) Brady. Being able to complete a high school education was a luxury because it meant that your family could survive without your labor, either at home or in the mines. By 1915, eight more young women had graduated. The first young men to receive diplomas did so in 1916. (93.13.6)

As more families moved to the area and began building a community together, celebrations became part of the social fabric. Pictured here *c.* 1915 are celebrants of the Fourth of July. (94.7.89D)

The Issaquah Valley Grange was organized in 1915. In 1916, this group of "grangers" attended a meeting at the Steel Lake (now known as Federal Way) Grange. Pictured, from left to right, are: (front row) William Pickering III, unidentified, Roy Pickering, Pete Erickson, unidentified, Art Tibbetts, and Gladys Bush; (back row) Hazel Bush, Orpha Lyne, Elmer Becker, Del Darst, Floyd Bush, Gladys Peterson, and Agnes Bush. (72.21.14.117)

The International Order of Odd Fellows (IOOF) chapter was established in 1888, the earliest lodge in the town. The IOOF Hall was built in the same year. In this 1900 photograph, the Gilman Coronet Band assembles in front of the building. (91.7.76)

Most of Gilman's (and later, Issaquah's) leading businessmen were members of the IOOF. When the lodge was officially founded in 1889, members included Andy Reynolds, superintendent of Grand Ridge Coal Mine, and Wilbur W. Sylvester. (2001.29.6)

The Issaquah Volunteer Fire Department (IVFD) was founded in 1912, formalizing the loose association of townspeople previously responsible for fighting fires. Pictured, from left to right, are the founding members, *c.* 1914: (front row) Fred Allen, Arthur Trigg, Walt Ek, and Leonard Miles; (middle row) Bill Schomber, Tom Evans, Jim Clark, Jack Hudson, Pete Favini, and Matt Yourglich; (back row) Frank "Lefty" Yourglich, Joe Edwards, George Clark, Charlie Thomas, Jim Croston, Jack Favini, Jack Tambourini, and Pete Donlan. (72.21.14.266)

Albin Ek's Place offered ice cream, candy, cigars, and soft drinks. It also provided the IVFD with a place to store their uniforms. When the fire alarm rang, volunteers would sprint into the sweet shop to change into their overalls, creating some excitement for Albin Ek's other patrons. Albin Ek stands in front of his store in this 1911 photograph. (72.21.14.51)

When not fighting fires, the IVFD also played on a baseball team they organized. Pictured, from left to right, in this team photograph, *c.* 1915, are: (front row) Johnny Kranik, Lawrence Harris, Jack Favini, and Dave Morgan; (middle row) Joe Yourglich, Blaine Boyden, Bert Hoye, Pete Favini, John Harris, and Alf Morris; (back row) Bill Schomber, Ed "Nogs" Seil, Bill Lindsey, (?) Thomas, Frank "Lefty" Yourglich, and Tom McQuade. (74.48.6)

This photograph, c. 1900, shows a view of Issaquah from the east. Power lines snake down the hill alongside Mill Street (today's Sunset Way). At the far left, Issaquah's first church, the First Methodist, is visible. In the lower right corner is St. Joseph's Catholic Church. Between the church and the depot is an empty field, part of which is destined to become today's Memorial Field. Members of the IVFD were instrumental in clearing this field for use by the community in the 1920s. (94.29.1)

Residents of the booming town did not have to wait long for streetlights and other electrical amenities—Issaquah had electricity even before Seattle. The Snoqualmie Power Company, Gilman Substation, was constructed on Mill Street (today's Sunset Way) in 1899. The town also had a privately owned water company, founded in 1888, and a telephone company, founded in 1900. (72.21.14.67)

In this photograph, *c.* 1905, workmen are either repairing or constructing wooden sidewalks in front of the Puget Power substation and the Grand Central Hotel. Wooden sidewalks were constructed on most downtown streets. The first concrete sidewalk was poured in 1910. In 1928, the City of Issaquah passed an ordinance requiring the use of cement for all future sidewalks. (89.2.3)

World War I dealt a blow to Alvo von Albensleben and the Issaquah and Superior Coal Company, contributing to the downturn in Issaquah's coal industry. It also cost the lives of Pete Erickson and Albert Larson. Pictured, from left to right, are Dave Clark, Floyd Lynn, and Joe Favini, who served in the Navy during World War I, and returned to Issaquah after the war. (74.48.2)

Vivian Ayers Hofto remembers a celebration at the end of the war: "Someone knew that Clifford [Vivian's brother Arthur Clifford Ayers, pictured here, c. 1918] had a soldier suit, so they bandaged his leg and arm, put a patch over a fake wound on his head, put him in a stretcher with four men carrying it down the street." The parade ended in the park where a straw effigy of Kaiser Wilhelm was burned. (2001.39.1)

This postcard view of Issaquah, c. 1910, shows what the town looked like to the incoming traveler. The depot is ahead and to the left is the Northwestern Milk Condensing Company. Stumps and a split rail fence are reminders of the forest, not long gone. Mount Rainier is visible from this angle, but only on clear days. The mountain was "enhanced" on this historic postcard to appear more picturesque. (93.32.1.60)

This holiday parade took place on Labor Day, c. 1915. The parade is moving south on Front Street, which is lined with cars and festooned with power lines. Beginning in the 1910s, community festivals became a strong part of Issaquah's community life. By the end of the decade, rodeos were to become a regular event. (72.21.14.163)

This rare panoramic photograph, c. 1912–1914, allows us to look down Front Street (at left) and Mill Street (today's Sunset Way, at right) at the same time. To the left, several men lounge outside the Pastime Saloon. Among the businesses on Front Street's right side, the distinctive

AT ISSAQUAH WASH

4205

false front of the IOOF Hall is visible. A rail spur leading to Mine Hill runs between the power line pole and the feed store. The depot itself is just beyond. (2002.25.1)

As mining declined, farming emerged as a major industry in Issaquah. This photograph was taken at Pickering Farm, c. 1910. The photograph was originally titled "Corn Country." The two men seem to be demonstrating the fertility of the land, and the hardiness of its produce. (86.18.268)

Even more than crops, Issaquah farms were known for their dairy production. The Pickering Dairy Farm thrived in the Issaquah Valley during the first half of the 20th century. This photograph of the farm was taken in 1911. William Pickering Sr., appointed as territorial governor by Abraham Lincoln, acquired the land in 1867 and established the farm. Pickering served as territorial governor from 1862 until 1866. (91.7.60C)

Henry Bergsma was the proprietor of the Issaquah Valley Dairy. His son, Bill Bergsma Sr., was a familiar sight as he delivered milk in the truck shown here. (86.18.273)

Issaquah's first car was shipped by rail and assembled in 1911. In this 1916 photograph, the Tibbetts and Goode families prepare for a car trip to Florida, more than 3,000 miles away. Pictured, from left to right, are Gertrude (Goode) McKinnon, George W. Tibbetts, Ida Maude (Goode) Walimaki, William Goode, Cora Bea (Goode) Lassen, Rebecca (Wilson) Tibbetts, Ida Mae (Tibbetts) Goode, John Maurice Goode, and Edward John Goode. (94.10.11)

The trip was probably a triumphal march as much as it was a family visit. George W. Tibbetts drafted the bill for a Snoqualmie Pass highway and pushed it through state legislature. The resulting gravel highway was the first to cross the Cascades. This postcard commemorates its opening in 1915. With the opening of the pass, Issaquah became a landmark on the path through the Cascades. (86.18.244)

54

While men like George W. Tibbetts saw the possibilities of cross-country automobile transportation, other practical minds saw the automobile as a rail alternative for short distances as well. After a short drive down the Sunset Highway, which opened in the early 1920s, passengers could board a ferry in Newport and reach Seattle by water. (90.32.1)

Issaquah's first stage line was the Issaquah-Coalfield-Renton Stage, providing service between these three communities. Pictured here, third from the left, is Tommy Gibson. Travel by rail from Issaquah to Seattle took roughly 2 hours; in 1914 the Issaquah-Renton-Seattle Stage advertised Issaquah-Seattle service in 1 hour and 10 minutes, with three round trips daily. By 1922, passenger service from Issaquah by rail was discontinued. (89.40.4)

Automobiles were also a viable option for freight service. The Issaquah & Seattle Freight Company was the earliest to haul freight between Issaquah and Seattle. As automobile transport became more readily available to families and businesses, the railroad became less critical to prosperity in Issaquah. (FIC.2000.46)

Two

ENJOYING A QUIET LIFE 1920–1960

After the initial boom of Issaquah's natural resource industries, life in Issaquah slowed to a more leisurely pace. In the 1920s, labor disputes at the mines had led to a decline in the coal industry. The Depression impacted the lumber industry as well. While logging continued to generate modest revenue, local logging towns like High Point and Monohon ceased to exist. Although dairy farming still thrived, Issaquah's days as a boomtown had come to a close.

Between 1920 and 1960, Issaquah's population fluctuated between 800 and 950 people. Photographs of Issaquah during this time period show a small, isolated, but nonetheless vibrant town with a close-knit population. Fraternal organizations like the Pythian Sisters and the Masonic Lodge provided important social outlets for the small community.

Long-time residents have fond memories of this era, marked by the Alpine Dairy football team's successive wins, the Squak Valley Hot Shots, and community celebrations like the rodeo and the Labor Day parade and carnival. Even World War II was described as a time when everyone pulled together as a team, holding rubber drives and taking shifts in the fire hall tower to look for enemy aircraft.

In 1940, the Lake Washington Floating Bridge opened. Few realized at the time what profound changes the bridge would bring about. Suddenly, Issaquah was not quite so far from the big city of Seattle as it had been. Issaquah's days as a small town would soon come to an end.

Photographs from 1920 to 1960 focus more on small-town life and recreation, rather than the elements of a booming mine and lumber town. This 1927 photograph of an "old-timer's" picnic takes place at Pine Lake. (89.13.34D)

Ice-skating at Horrocks' Farm was a popular winter pastime for several generations of Issaquah residents. (2001.36.1)

These photographs are from the collection of Minnie Wilson Schomber, a well-known teacher for several generations of students. Minnie also served as the town clerk in the 1930s. Minnie and her husband Jake were avid outdoorsmen, who enjoyed hunting and fishing. Her diaries contain details of their frequent duck hunting trips, and the resulting dinners. Pictured above, from left to right, are Jake and Minnie Schomber with their hunting dogs and a brace of ducks. The man in the photograph at right is unidentified. (94.7.10B, above, and 94.7.10A, at right)

This 1931 photograph shows, from left to right, Bob Alma, J. Hooker Hailstone, and Joe Haldeman ready to go camping with their rifles. In the background is Hooker Hailstone's 1931 Chevy Roadster, described by him as a beauty, maroon in color with a black top. (2001.29.3)

In 1921, the City of Issaquah acquired land to form a park. This picture of the Issaquah Free Camp Ground was taken c. 1926–1927. The park was a popular site for picnics and outings. Since then, the City Park has been cut in half by Newport Way; Gibson Hall is located on the west side, and the Issaquah Salmon Hatchery is on the east side. (93.26.3)

Commencement = Program
Issaquah High School
June 8, 1921

Music _____ "Glad Summer Sun" _____ Glee Club
Invocation _____ Rev. Nicholl
Salutatory _____ "Immigration" _____ Lulu Peterson
Solo _____ "The Star" _____ Ferol Tibbetts
Oration _____ "America's Opportunity" _____ Robert Morgan
Music _____ "Flying Clouds" _____ Glee Club
Reading _____ "The World's All Right" _____ Dorothy Hailstone
Valedictory __ "The Life and Works of Dante" __ Marie Barlow
Address _____ "Peptimist" _____ E. J. Klemme
Class Song _____ Glee Club
Presentation of Diplomas _____ A. L. Wold
Member of Board of Education
Benediction _____ Rev. Nicholl

Class Roll

BARLOW, MARIE	McEACHERN, SARA
BONI, ANGELO	PECK, PEARL
HAILSTONE, DOROTHY	PETERSON, LULU
HARRIS, JOHN	SCHOMBER, GERTRUDE
HAYWARD, MARY	SCOTT, REGINALD
JUSSILA, WAINO	SKOGMAN, FLORENCE
KRANICK, KATE	SWEEN, ALIX
MARCHETTE, ALLIE	THOMPSON, MILDRED
MORGAN, ROBERT	TIBBETTS, FEROL

This 1921 Issaquah High Commencement Program celebrates the graduation of 18 students. Several pioneer names, such as Tibbetts and Wold, appear on the program. (91.5.1)

During the 1920s, local merchants closed their stores to attend the popular Friday night Issaquah High School football games. The University of Washington donated their old purple and gold uniforms, establishing Issaquah High's trademark colors. Pictured from left to right in this 1926 photograph are: (front row) Silvio Monte, George Kinnune, Clarence Palm, John Kramer, Hugo Lundquist, and Floyd Erickson; (back row) Paul Kinnune, Homer Hallworth, Harold Erickson, William Yourglich, Orval Garner, and (?) Shobart. (2001.7.1)

The Issaquah High women's basketball team, founded in 1912, wore restrictive uniforms consisting of bloomers, black stockings, and white middy blouses. This uniform did not change until the late 1920s. Pictured, from left to right, are 1921 team members: (front row) Erma Brown, Marie Chevalier, and Julia Erickson; (back row) May Wilkinson, Alix Sween, Pearl Peck, Alene O'Connor, and Mildred Thompson. (FIC.2000.49)

Issaquah High School offered opportunities for young thespians as well as athletes. This 1927 photograph shows the drama club in gypsy costumes. Pictured, from left to right, are: (front row) Gertrude Castagno, Betty Beck, Bess Mamie Maness, Harold Kehoe, Clara Johnson, (?) Kangas, Esther Garner, Ann Monti, Alice Lundquist, and Sofie Walen; (middle row) Annie Boehm, Steve Krall, Margaret Lindsay, Ethel Isotalo, May Lindstrom, Hilding Halvanson, and Harry Pearson; (back row) Ferol Tibbetts, George Kinnune, Svea Zingmark, Alvin Kerola, Elma Erickson, Florence Jones, Ruby Lundquist, Helen Smith, Thelma Olsen, Lila Erickson, Doris Zingmark, Esther Erickson, Thelma Bush, Clarence Palm, Algot Nygren, and Albert Karvia. (2002.20.1)

INCORPORATED UNDER THE LAWS OF
WASHINGTON
Nº
Shares — Ten —

ISSAQUAH PLAYFIELD ASSOCIATION

ISSAQUAH, WASHINGTON

This Certifies that _____ A. L. Wold _____ is the owner of
_____ Ten _____ Shares of the Capital Stock of

transferable only on the books of the Corporation by the holder hereof in person or by Attorney, upon surrender of this certificate properly endorsed.

In Witness Whereof, the said Corporation has caused this Certificate to be signed by its duly authorized officers and to be sealed with the seal of the Corporation this _____ day of _____ A.D. 19__

SECRETARY   PRESIDENT

$10.00 EACH

Throughout the 1920s, the biggest celebration in Issaquah was undoubtedly the rodeo. The Playfield Association, a group of local businessmen, sponsored the rodeo as a fundraiser, in the hope that they would be able to buy out interest in Memorial Field. *Issaquah Press* articles from this time period indicate that for many years the Association barely broke even. (FIC.2002.17)

The Issaquah Round-up was held on July 4th weekends from roughly 1923 until at least 1931. A man from Calgary, Canada, known as "Strawberry Red" Wall, managed the rodeo company, which traveled on a circuit. In this picture, Rose Wall (probably Wall's wife or daughter) competes. (87.150.23A)

Most of the rodeo events featured seasoned rodeo riders like this man, who rode the circuit. However, in 1928 the Issaquah businessmen's race gave locals a chance to compete. The following were listed in the *Issaquah Press* as competitors in this race: Edmiston, Clark, Fischer, Lundberg, Peters, Miles, and Wold. (72.21.14.264A)

Women competed in several events designed specifically for "the cowgirls." In 1926, Mrs. Mike Stewart also earned a mention in the *Issaquah Press*, being the first woman to act as pick-up man at the rodeo. The pick-up man's job was to pluck a successful rider from his mount while the horse was still bucking or running. Pictured, left to right, are Reva (?) and Rose Wall. (87.150.23D)

65

Annual rodeo events included chariot races, wild horse races, steer wrestling, calf roping, and bareback riding. There are several theories concerning the demise of the rodeo: one involved lack of profit, and the other was that Mayor Stella Alexander put an end to the rodeo because of its unsavory influences. By 1931 it seemed that the rodeo was in definite financial trouble. The Playfield Association had arranged to have "Strawberry Red" Wall take over the costs of promoting the show, leaving the Association to take on only the risk of the concession sales. (87.150.23B, above, and 87.150.23C, below)

Elected in 1932, Stella Alexander was Issaquah's first female mayor, and a decidedly controversial figure. Some speculate that her assertiveness would have been better tolerated if she had been a man. In one incident, three councilmen refused to serve under a "petticoat mayor." Alexander appointed new councilmen. Two groups of councilmen arrived at the next meeting. When no one supported her motion to have one group leave, Alexander settled the manner by brandishing a chair. (72.21.14.274).

Stella Alexander is shown below at her installation. In another incident during her tenure, she demanded that the Issaquah Volunteer Fire Department put out fires only within city limits. As a result, the IVFD resigned, resentful of this restriction on their powers to put out fires wherever the need arose. Remo Castagno, the fire chief, was quoted as saying, "No woman is going to run this city." In 1934, Alexander was recalled from office. (72.21.14.276)

Les Adair remembers earning extra money during the Depression: "I managed to pay for most of my school expenses and clothes with money that I earned trapping mink, muskrat, skunk, weasel. One skunk hide earned $7.50." Lawrence Campbell took this photograph of pelts drying in the 1930s; he and friend Dave Bonner trapped muskrat and skunk together. (2001.31.2)

Other local residents worked for the Works Project Administration, which provided jobs replacing the Issaquah sewer and water systems and constructing facilities like Gibson Hall, the Sportsmen's Club, and the Issaquah Salmon Hatchery. The hatchery was constructed during 1936 and 1937. During recent renovation, this graffiti was found on an interior board: "Magnus Sellberg, High Point Sept. 17, 1936, USWPA. This was the way we had of existing thru happy days of capitalism." (72.21.14.41A)

The Depression took a toll on Issaquah's lumber economy. Although many mills continued to operate, production slowed. This photograph of the Issaquah Lumber Company was taken in the summer of 1931. Pictured from left to right are Lester Adair, Edvin Erickson, Martin Hanson, Joe Hanson, Erick Erickson Jr., Tim Evans, Nils Bergvall, Carl Berntsen, Floyd Erickson, Carl Pearson, Fred Franzeen, Albin Hedberg, and Roy Hedberg. (86.18.235)

A field trip, c. 1945, took school children to visit the lumber operations still underway in Snoqualmie. (2000.18.3)

The Issaquah Lumber crew is shown here in the planer shed at its Monohon mill, c. 1943. Shown here are Floyd Erickson (third from left), and his father Erick Erickson Sr., the mill's owner (fourth from the left). Other unidentified subjects are members of the Rudstrom family, including several women who stepped in to help during World War II. (91.17.5)

Pictured here is James Matson, logging boss at the Preston Mill Company in the 1920s. Preston was one of the few outlying logging towns that continued to thrive after the Depression. Monohon's heyday ended with the 1925 fire and High Point's logging camps burned in 1922. (92.28.6)

Classes were held at the Preston School until 1965, when the school closed and students from the Preston area began attending Clark Elementary in Issaquah. Pictured from left to right are: (front row) Lola Mathews, Vickie DeBoer, Mary Erickson, Marlene Risen, and Brenda (?); (middle row) Roger Johanson, Wayne Fredeen, Lowell Pratt, Charles Elven, Harold (?), Harold Mallare, Gene Davis, and Susan Ackerman; (back row) teacher Marian Oules, Nadine Mallare, JoAnne O'Berg, Laverne Howatson, Lola Pearson, Dolly Ward, June Mathews, Glenda Duclos, and Eleanor Johanson. (72.21.14.22A)

Preston was founded and settled by Swedes, and the community continues to celebrate its Swedish heritage. The Order of Vasa is a fraternal organization honoring Swedish heritage. This photograph commemorates the opening of the new Vasa Hall in Upper Preston in 1950. (92.28.8)

Dairy farming was a major industry during the middle part of the 20th century. A group of school children stand in front of the Bergsma barn, c. 1950. The Bergsma family operated the Issaquah Valley Dairy from 1912 until 1969. (2001.38.2)

In this photograph from the 1950s, Bill Bergsma Sr. poses in front of the Issaquah Junior High School with some students. The presence of both milk and athletic equipment implies that the picture is a promotion, driving home the message that milk builds healthy, athletic bodies. Pictured, from left to right, are Bill Bergsma Sr., Duane Marberg, Leon Cooke, Gary Baugh, Steve Johnson, and Marianne Boncutter. (72.21.14.66B)

In 1909, dairy farmer John Anderson founded the Northwestern Milk Condensing Company, which became the Alpine Dairy Company in the 1930s. A number of small farms sold milk to Alpine, which produced and distributed a variety of dairy products. Alpine also sponsored the town football team. Pictured, from left to right, are Everett Harrington, Gordon Crosby, Carl Walker, Jake Borman, Rod Anderson, and Keith Pickering in front of the Alpine Dairy, c. 1950. (72.21.14.66A)

Farming remained a viable career option for Issaquah High graduates, as evidenced by the presence of a strong local chapter of the Future Farmers of America (FFA). This FFA chapter flourished for over 30 years under the supervision of advisor Fred Frohs. Pictured above, from right to left, are the 1948 FFA members: (front row) Howard Carlin, Bud Hyatt, Larry Bernert, and Bob Nightingale; (back row) Dave Watson, Ron Howatson, Basil Bakamus, Lloyd Larson, Ken Wallace, Orville Anderson, Bill Padden, John Ronney, Don Thompson, Jack Barker, Art Dolan, and Fred Frohs. Pictured below, from left to right, are the FFA officers from 1952 to 1953: Ewing Stringfellow, Bill Bergsma Jr., Tim Ballard, George Kritsonis, and Alonzo Kinney. (97.15.1, above, and 97.15.2, below)

In this picture, the 1939 Alpine Dairy football team poses on Memorial Field shortly after a game. Pictured, from left to right, are: (front row) unidentified, Paul Knoernschild, Elsworth Croston, unidentified, (?) Hume, unidentified, and Merv Castagno; (middle row) Bill Rowe, Jim Marenakos, Roy Schultz, Truman Hume, unidentified, Carl Walker, unidentified, and unidentified; (back row) Ted Stonebridge, Irv Dalbotten, George Reini, unidentified, Tony Walen, Ed Parker, Bill Castagno, Silvio Brolio, John Castagno, unidentified, unidentified, and unidentified. (2001.7.14)

The Issaquah High School football team looks poised for action in this 1941 photograph. Chuck Fallstrom, third from the left (in dark suit) was the team's assistant coach that year; he would later become the high school principal. Both the Alpine team and the Issaquah High School team had their ranks thinned when many young men left to fight in World War II. (2001.27.2)

Wilbur Pickering was one of many young men in Issaquah who enlisted to serve their country during World War II. The wings pinned to his chest and the emblems on his lapel signify that he was probably a Marine paratrooper. (94.21.16)

This photograph, c. 1945, shows the Hayes family helping with a rubber drive for the war effort. Marian Hampton remembers, "We planted Victory Gardens and pasted stamps in books to buy War Bonds. . . . We were all focused on one thing and it was winning the war. It was the last time I can remember when there was no dissension." Pictured, from front to back, are James Hayes, Don Hayes, John Hayes Jr., and John Hayes Sr. (2001.30.2)

During the war Issaquah residents took turns watching for enemy aircraft from the tower of the Issaquah Volunteer Fire Department building. Linda Adair Hjelm remembers, "My grandmother [Charlotte "Chattie" Adair] and I went on air raid watches. . . . I remember vividly looking south down the valley, totally baffled that this word 'war' I kept hearing could possibly invade the air space above my safe home." (72.21.14.250)

Issaquah lost 12 young men and women in World War II. They were Alfred Ambrose, Robert Baskett, Clifford Benson, Elizabeth Erickson, Harold Gleason, George Larsen, Laurence Lortie, Jack McQuade, Louis Petersen, Robert Philip, Raymond Smart, Joe Tondreau, and Robert Watson. This honor guard for the Veterans of Foreign Wars marched in the Labor Day parade in their honor, c. 1949–1950. (2001.34.1)

Sec. 562, P. L. & R.
Permit No. 14
U. S.
POSTAGE PAID
ISSAQUAH, WASH.

Coming Programs at The
ISSAQUAH THEATRE

Latest News
and
Selected Shorts
with
Each Program

Sunday show continuous from 4:30. Two shows Mon., Wed., Thur., Fri. and Sat., starting at 6:45. Dark on Tuesday

ADMISSION: ADULTS 40c, SERVICEMEN (in Uniform) 30c, CHILDREN (under 12) 15c, Including Taxes

---

SUN.-MON., MAY 12, 13—

"SENTIMENTAL JOURNEY"

with

JOHN PAYNE, MAUREEN O'HARA, WILLIAM BENDIX

Color Cartoon . . News

SUN.-MON., MAY 19, 20—

in Technicolor

"THE BANDIT OF SHERWOOD FOREST"

with

CORNELL WILDE

Disney Cartoon
Sports & News

SUN.-MON., MAY 26, 27—

"UP GOES MAISIE"

with

ANN SOTHERN and GEORGE MURPHY

Color Cartoon and News

Special: See Nelson and McSpaden
play their irons

SUN.-MON., JUNE 2, 3—

"THEY WERE EXPENDABLE"

with

ROBERT MONTGOMERY, JOHN WAYNE, DONNA REED

NOTE: First Show Sunday at 3:30
Feature Time—3:45, 6:20 and 8:50

SUN.-MON., JUNE 9, 10—

in Technicolor

"THE HARVEY GIRLS"

with

JUDY GARLAND and JOHN HODIAK

Color Cartoon and News

SUN.-MON., JUNE 16, 17—

JUNE ALLYSON and ROBERT WALKER
in

"THE SAILOR TAKES A WIFE"

TIMBERLAND ATHLETES
Cartoon and News

WED.-THURS., MAY 15, 16—

DOROTHY LAMOUR

and

JOHN HALL

in

"HURRICANE"

News

WED.-THURS., MAY 22, 23—

in Technicolor

"YOLANDA AND THE THIEF"

with

LUCILLE BREMER, FRED ASTAIRE,

and

FRANK MORGAN

News

WED.-THURS., MAY 29, 30—

"WHAT NEXT, CORPORAL HARGROVE?"

with

ROBERT WALKER, JEAN PORTER, KEENAN WYNN

Hi Ho Rodeo and News

WED.-THURS., JUNE 5, 6—

MARSHA HUNT

and

JOHN CARROLL

in

"A LETTER FOR EVIE"

Cartoon and News

WED.-THURS., JUNE 12, 13—

"THE DARK CORNER"

with

LUCILLE BALL

and

WILLIAM BENDIX

Cartoon and News

WED.-THURS., JUNE 19, 20—

"VACATION FROM MARRIAGE"

with

ROBERT DONAT and DEBORAH KERR

News
Film Vodvil

FRI.-SAT., MAY 17, 18 — DOUBLE FEATURE

ROY ROGERS and TRIGGER

in

"SONG OF ARIZONA"

and

JAMES CRAIG and SIGNE HASSO

in

"DANGEROUS PARTNERS"

FRI.-SAT., MAY 24, 25 — DOUBLE FEATURE

The WEAVER BROS. and ELVIRY

in

"MOUNTAIN MOONLIGHT"

and

GEORGE O'BRIEN

in

"MARSHAL OF MESA CITY"

Color Cartoon

FRI.-SAT., MAY 31, JUNE 1—

So good you'll want to see it again

Walt Disney's

"PINOCCHIO"

in Technicolor

El Brendel Comedy and "Canine Champions"

FRI.-SAT., JUNE 7, 8 — DOUBLE FEATURE

RED RYDER, LITTLE BEAVER
and THE DUCHESS in

"PHANTOM OF THE PLAINS"

and LAUREL & HARDY in

"JITTERBUGS"

Color Cartoon

FRI.-SAT., JUNE 14, 15—DOUBLE FEATURE

"OH SUSANNA"

with GENE AUTRY and SMILEY BURNETTE

and a thrilling story of the ice

"GAY BLADES"

Also Disney's "PLUTO'S KID BROTHER"

FRI.- SAT., JUNE 21, 22—

"ABILENE TOWN"

with

RANDOLPH SCOTT and ANN DVORAK

also

Three Stooges Comedy and Color Cartoon

Even after the war's end, reminders persisted. Movies with a military theme, like *What Next, Corporal Hargrove?* and *The Sailor Takes a Wife*, were popular at the Issaquah Theatre. Servicemen in uniform were also given a theatre discount, a mark of respect for the men who had so recently risked their lives. This Issaquah Theatre flyer is c. 1946. (2000.26.91)

After the rodeo came to a close in the 1930s, Labor Day became the town's chief celebration. The first Labor Day festivities were held in 1936. This 1952 float was the first to adopt a Native American theme, borrowing from the Issaquah High mascot. Pictured, from left to right, are Joan Hayes, Liz Njos, Claudia Miles, Lynora Lynn Reeves, Delores Santa, LaDonna Hansen, and Hazel Blakeslee. (72.21.14.258)

Labor Day celebrations featured a parade down Front Street on Monday, the last day of the festivities. Early Labor Day programs also included celebrity speeches, foot and bike races, horseshoe games, and scout demonstrations. In this photograph, c. 1941, the Issaquah High School band leads the parade. The majorettes in the lead are, from left to right: (front row) Anna Marie Favini, Shirley Peterson, and Rae Castagno; (back row) Betty Sutter, unidentified, and Faye (Harrington) Linderoth. (2002.26.1)

By the 1950s and 1960s, Labor Day festivities became more elaborate. Fancy floats, a children's parade, beauty queens, drill team performances, and truck rodeos became features of the holiday festivities. An evening carnival brought rides, games, and carnival workers to town. In this parade, c. the 1950s, members of the poodle act included Karen Sandberg, Debbie Pettite, Alona Pettite, Sandy Pettite, Judy Colausurdo, and Kathy Anderson. (72.21.14.257A)

This elaborate float, hosted by Tony and Johnnie's Food Center, Nick's Café, and Fischer's Market, features two "dog butchers" brandishing knives. The real butchers here are actually the men in white coats to the right. From left to right are town butchers Ai Garner, Nick Fischer, and George Fischer, cooking up hot dogs to be served to the crowd. (2001.7.6)

Labor Day Queens were chosen based on the largest number of ticket sales supporting a particular candidate. This tradition evolved into the Miss Issaquah competition in the late 1960s. In this 1953 photograph, Arline Nikko's family gathers around the recently crowned Labor Day Queen. Arline (in center, wearing tiara) is holding hands with Floyd Hefferline, who would later become her husband. (2001.22.3)

In this 1952 Labor Day photograph, "criminals" (from left to right) Dorothy "Sunny" Hailstone, Candy Hailstone, Don Hooker Hailstone, and J. Hooker Hailstone peer at us from behind bars. They were convicted of a crime common in the town during Labor Day festivities. Anyone caught without a beard was put in jail and was not released until bail, a hefty $1, was paid. (2001.29.1)

Local organizations and lodges were enthusiastic participants in the Labor Day celebrations. The parade in particular was an opportunity for groups to express themselves. This Issaquah Grange float, c. 1950, has a Dutch theme, complete with windmill and tulips. (72.21.14.259E)

The Gilman Rebekah Lodge No. 59 was one of several fraternal organizations for women. Founded in 1893, it was an auxiliary to the International Order of Odd Fellows. Pictured in this photograph, c. 1937, from left to right, are: (front row) Isabel Eaves, Mabel Miles, Emily Walker, Ruby Lindman, and Walcie Kramer; (back row) Velma Lewis, Esther Thompson, Velma Anderson, Gladys Brown, and Elsie Matilla. (2000.18.5)

84

The Pythian Sisters were an auxiliary group to the Knights of Pythias. They held their meetings in the IOOF Hall. The Pythian Sisters made a regular appearance in Labor Day parades. Pictured, from left to right, are: (front row) unidentified, unidentified, and Kay McElfresh; (back row) Charlotte "Chattie" Adair, Ilene Pennington, Ada (Bonner) Seil, and Rita (?). (72.21.14.259A)

The Squak Valley Hot Shots were an all-women's folk band that grew out of the Pythian Sisters. In this Labor Day parade, c. 1950, Elinor Munden plays guitar while accompanied on the washboard. (2001.32.3)

Not only were the Squak Valley Hot Shots a much-anticipated part of the Labor Day festivities—they were also recording artists! The homegrown group produced at least one 45 rpm recording in their career. The Squak Valley Hot Shots in this 1947 photograph are, from left to right, Madge Brundage, Kay McElfresh, Charlotte "Chattie" Adair, Elinor Munden, Beryl Nelson, and Ilene Pennington. (72.21.14.145)

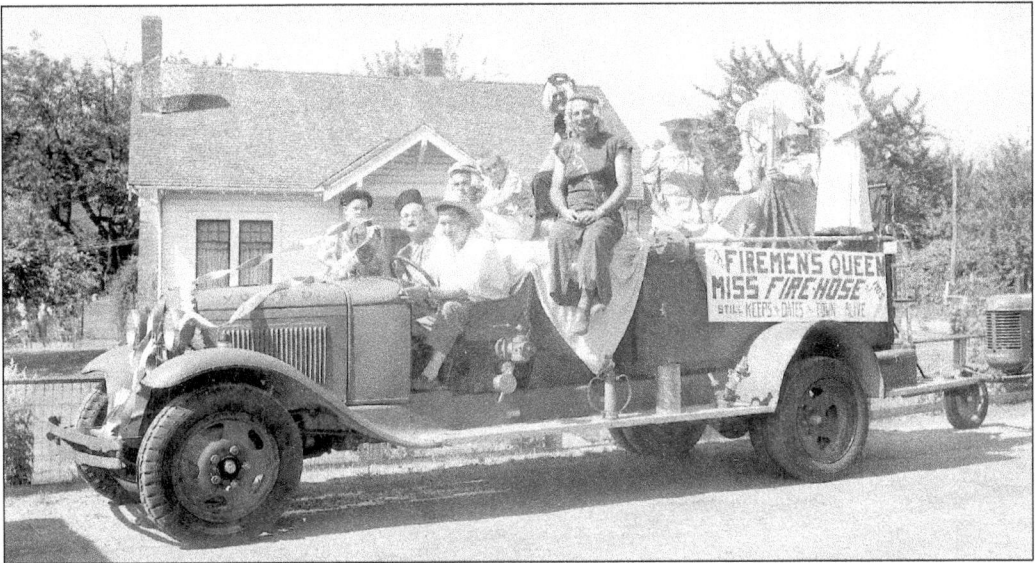

Labor Day festivities were a time for laughter and outrageous jokes. In this photograph, *c.* the 1940s, members of the Issaquah Volunteer Fire Department, in drag, celebrate "Miss Firehose of 1905," who "Still keeps her dates and town alive." Pictured in the driver's seat, from left to right, are: unidentified, Gordon Crosby, and Claude Brown. Don Anderson is in the foreground wearing a blonde wig. Reclining in back is Miss Firehose, Joe Chevalier. (72.21.14.265B)

The Issaquah Volunteer Fire Department were dedicated men, serious when it came to fighting fires. The IVFD remained an all-volunteer department until 1972. Pictured, from left to right, *c.* 1950, are: (front row) Earl Lindsay, Stan Favini, Bill Doherty, Bob Beach, Roy Croston, and Steve Somsak; (middle row) Don Anderson, Howard McQuade, Roy Schultz, Ernie Nyberg, and Joe Chevalier; (back row) Claude Brown, Gordon Crosby, Jeff Lindquist, Ray Spjut, Merv Castagno, and Gary Mitchell. (72.21.14.248B)

This image depicts Front Street, c. 1950–1954. The scene captures the all-American appeal of Issaquah's downtown area during the 1950s. At left is the Union Tavern; on the right is Wold's Hardware Store. Businesses in Issaquah continued to grow, slowly but steadily, during the 1950s. (72.21.14.87)

The Grange Mercantile Association offered a variety of goods to Issaquah residents, including garden tools, feed, and hardware. There were also frozen meat lockers for food storage. In this 1937 photograph, a line of children and attendants wait outside the Grange Mercantile building in preparation for the Labor Day children's parade. The Issaquah Valley Grange founded the Mercantile in 1916. (72.21.14.158A)

Lou and Gertie Lawill ran Lawill's Drug Store on Front Street. Long-time residents recall purchasing everything from comic books and candy to gifts and medication at the store. Notice the sign for Alpine ice cream in the bottom right corner of this 1951 photograph. Gertie and Lou Lawill stand behind the counter. (72.21.14.129)

The grocery store in this 1931 photograph was operated by the Finnish Talus family, and was a gathering place for Finnish community members. Issaquah's Finnish community was significant; at one time they had their own church. There was also a Finnish Community Club in Issaquah. Pictured, from left to right, are John Talus, Mary Talus, Saima Wright, and Bill Wright. (72.21.14.73)

In addition to operating the Victory Inn Café on Front Street, Bill Hartley also served as town marshal from 1942 until 1945. In this photograph, c. 1945, Hartley (second from right) and his family sit in the Café together. Other popular eateries of the era included the Shamrock and the XXX. (94.21.10)

John Chevalier (left) and Elmer Huvinen are pictured here in the Union Tavern, founded in 1937. Signs inside the bar demonstrate the character of its proprietors: "If your family needs your money, we don't want your business" and "Let's be sociable without any profanity." Sue Bush Cameron remembers, "When I turned 21 my mom took me to the Union Tavern. They would give you this very large mug on your birthday and everyone kept it filled. Need I say more?" (72.21.14.38)

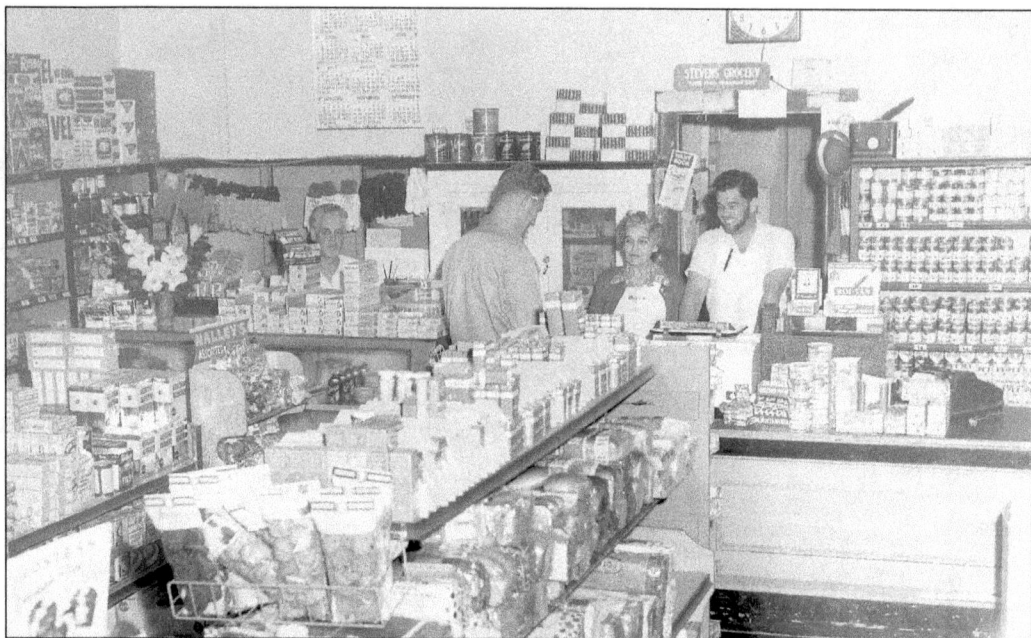

Stevens' Grocery Store was located in the IOOF Hall on Front Street, and had a pot-bellied stove. Pictured in 1951, from left to right, are Harry Stevens, unidentified, Rae Stevens, and Robert Stevens. Tony and Johnnie's and the Red and White were other popular grocery stores at the time. (72.21.14.65C)

By the 1950s, enough Issaquah residents owned cars that Cal Hood could find a market for automotive supplies. In this photograph from 1951, Cal Hood (at left, in suspenders) assists customers at Hood's Auto Parts. (72.21.14.65B)

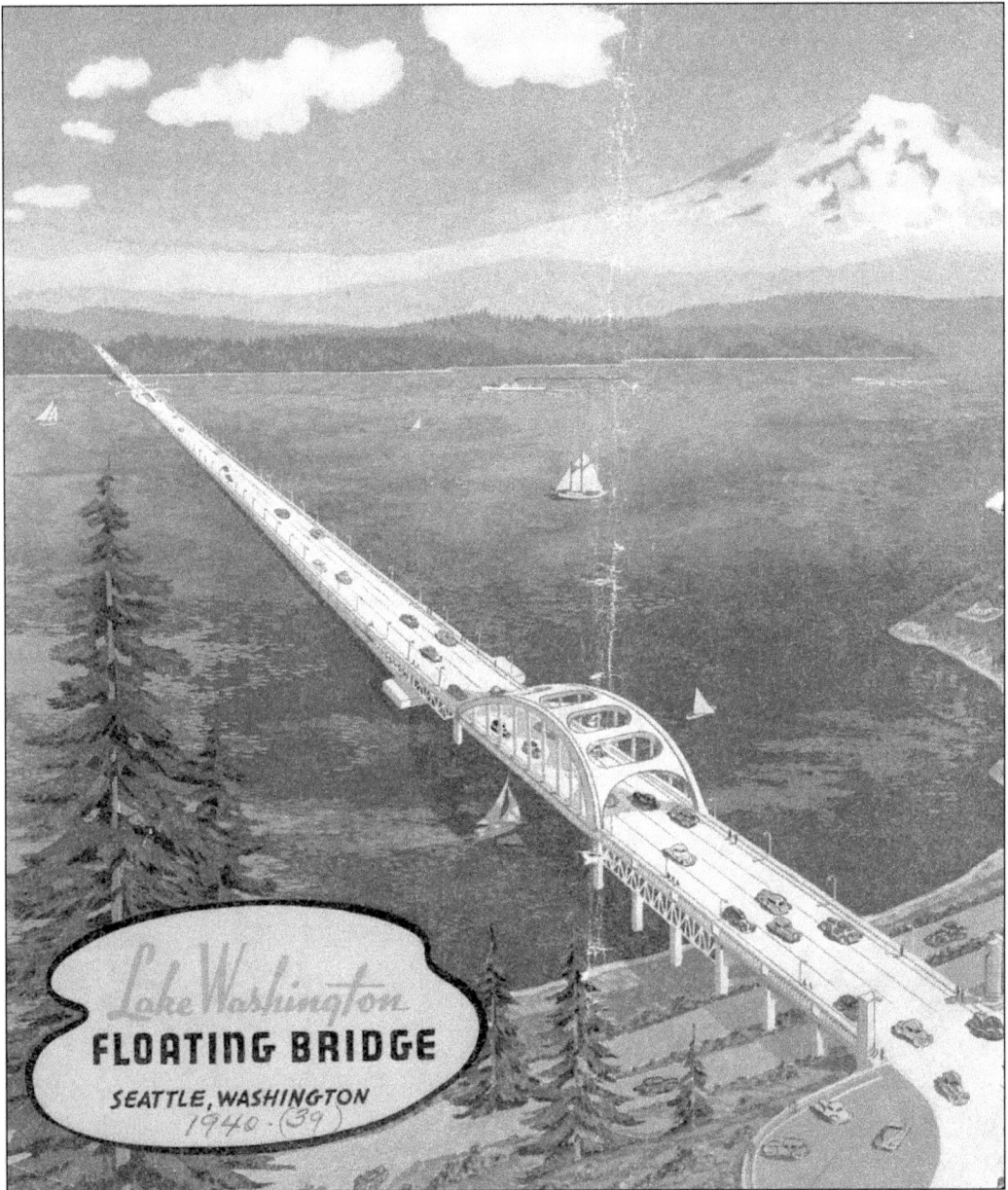

Lake Washington
FLOATING BRIDGE
SEATTLE, WASHINGTON
1940 - (39)

Although photographs from this era seem to show the town of Issaquah as small and timeless, by the 1950s change was already occurring. The Lake Washington Floating Bridge, the first bridge across the lake, opened in 1940. This new path dramatically shortened the time needed to get from Issaquah to Seattle. The opening of the bridge meant that more Issaquah residents could find employment in Seattle—and that more Seattle residents could move to the east side of Lake Washington and still commute to work. During the 1950s, Seattle's population dropped from 700,000 to 550,000 as a migration to the suburbs began. This program is a souvenir of the bridge's dedication ceremony, held July 2, 1940. (74.9.161)

Along with the bridge came a new highway, Highway 10. Part of this highway is now Gilman Boulevard. The bridge and highway, in tandem, were intended to provide a traffic route from the trading center of the Puget Sound, across Lake Washington and the Cascades, and on to points east. This 1941 aerial view of Issaquah shows the path of Highway 10 through the valley's farmland. (91.32.1)

The construction of Highway 10 required the relocation or demolition of several old Issaquah homes. The Baxter home, shown here in 1940, was one of those in the highway's path. Highway 10 also divided several family dairy farms in the area, including the Barlow farm, the Bergsma farm, and the Pickering farm. (73.43.15)

As automobiles met more transportation needs, the railroad industry declined. In 1958, the Issaquah Depot closed down. Trains continued to service the dairy and the quarry, but freight service from the depot was no longer available. Pictured above is the Issaquah trestle, with an eastbound freight train. Pictured at right, c. 1955, is Don Currie, Issaquah's last station agent. Currie is demonstrating the use of an order hoop, used by station agents to pass messages to moving trains. (94.30.1, above, and 72.21.14.301, at right)

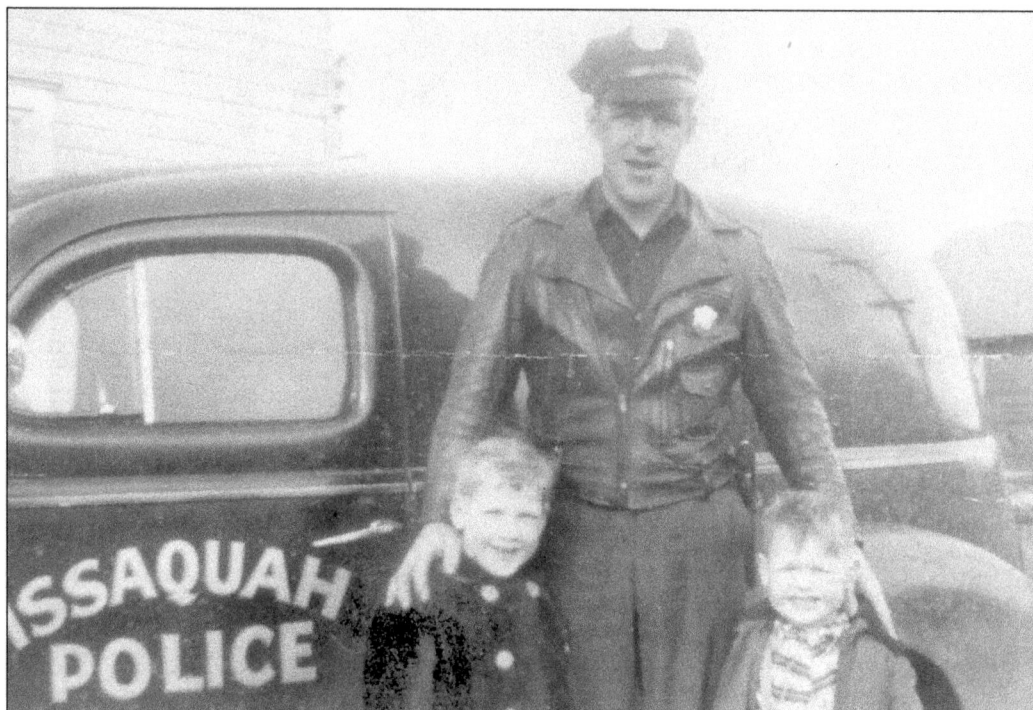

Issaquah town marshal Ray Robertson was instrumental in purchasing the city's first police department squad car at what he considered a surprisingly affordable price. Robertson remembers, " . . . That Ford would do 87 mph in second gear! Those country boys never beat me." Robertson also believed that all law enforcement workers should wear uniforms. In this 1949 photograph, he poses in front of the squad car with his two children. (72.21.14.241)

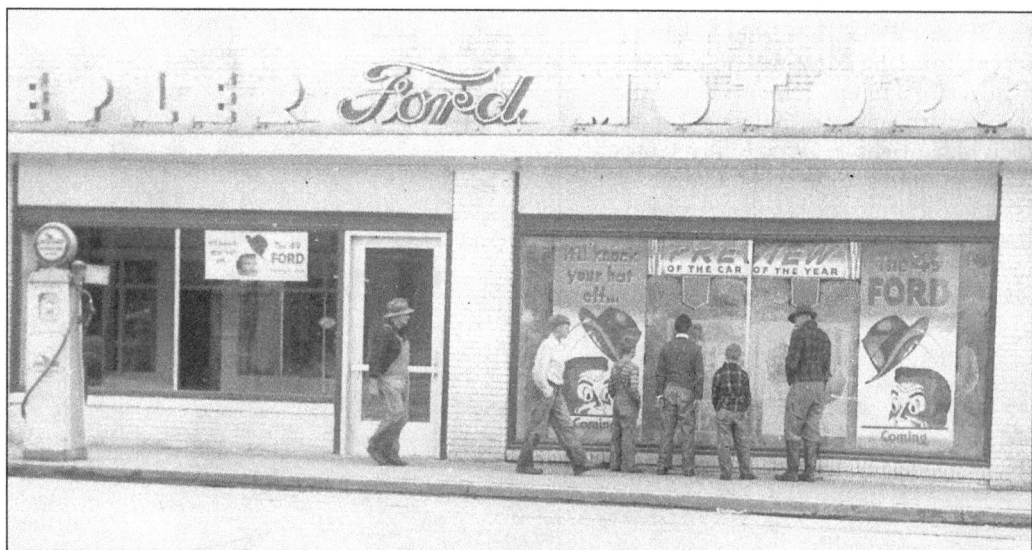

Automobiles weren't just for the wealthy anymore, and most families could afford one. In this 1948 photograph, Issaquah residents crowd the front window of Hepler Ford to see the 1949 model. Lee Hepler, a former Issaquah mayor, ran the Ford dealership. He was known for his ads in the *Issaquah Press*, frequent radio spots, and gala events, all of which helped sell cars. (72.21.14.59)

Like Cal Hood of Hood's Auto Parts, these two proprietors of City Auto discovered that there was money to be made in the repair and maintenance of cars. Pictured in this 1951 photograph, from left to right, are Alex Strnard and Dick Berntsen, who worked for Hepler Ford for 20 years before opening their own business. City Auto was often referred to simply as "Dick and Alex's." (72.21.14.64A)

Gib's Tire and Service, pictured here c. 1944, was another business built with the growing popularity of the automobile in mind. (94.21.6)

This view, c. 1951, greeted travelers entering Issaquah from the east via the Sunset Way. (72.21.14.235)

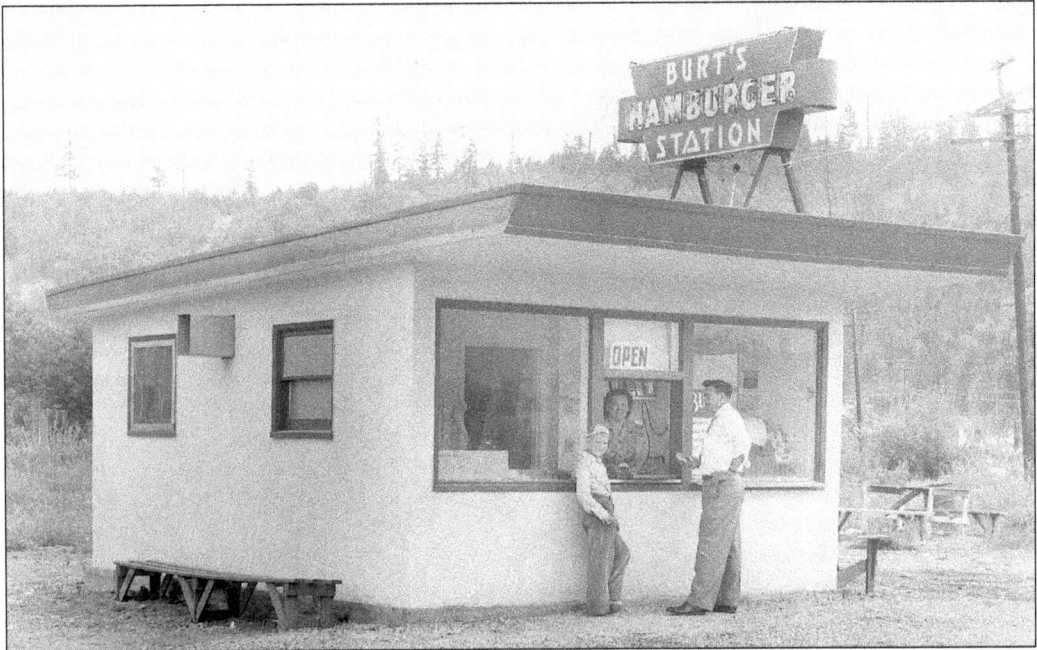

With the increase in auto travel came drive-through restaurants and roadside attractions. Burt's Hamburger Station on Highway 10 (today's Gilman Boulevard) catered to travelers looking for a quick bite to eat. Pictured here in 1951 are, from left to right, Roy, Mabel, and Clarence Burt, proprietors. Clarence and Mabel Burt started the roadside burger business in 1950 on the spot where the Pogacha Restaurant stands in 2002. (72.21.14.71)

Julius Boehm established Boehm's Candy in 1951. The shop was on Highway 10, down the road from Burt's, and it became a popular stop for travelers passing through Issaquah on their way to or from the Cascades. Boehm was a sports enthusiast who scaled Mount Rainier in 1979, at the age of 80. His candy store continues to please the public in 2002. (2002.27.16)

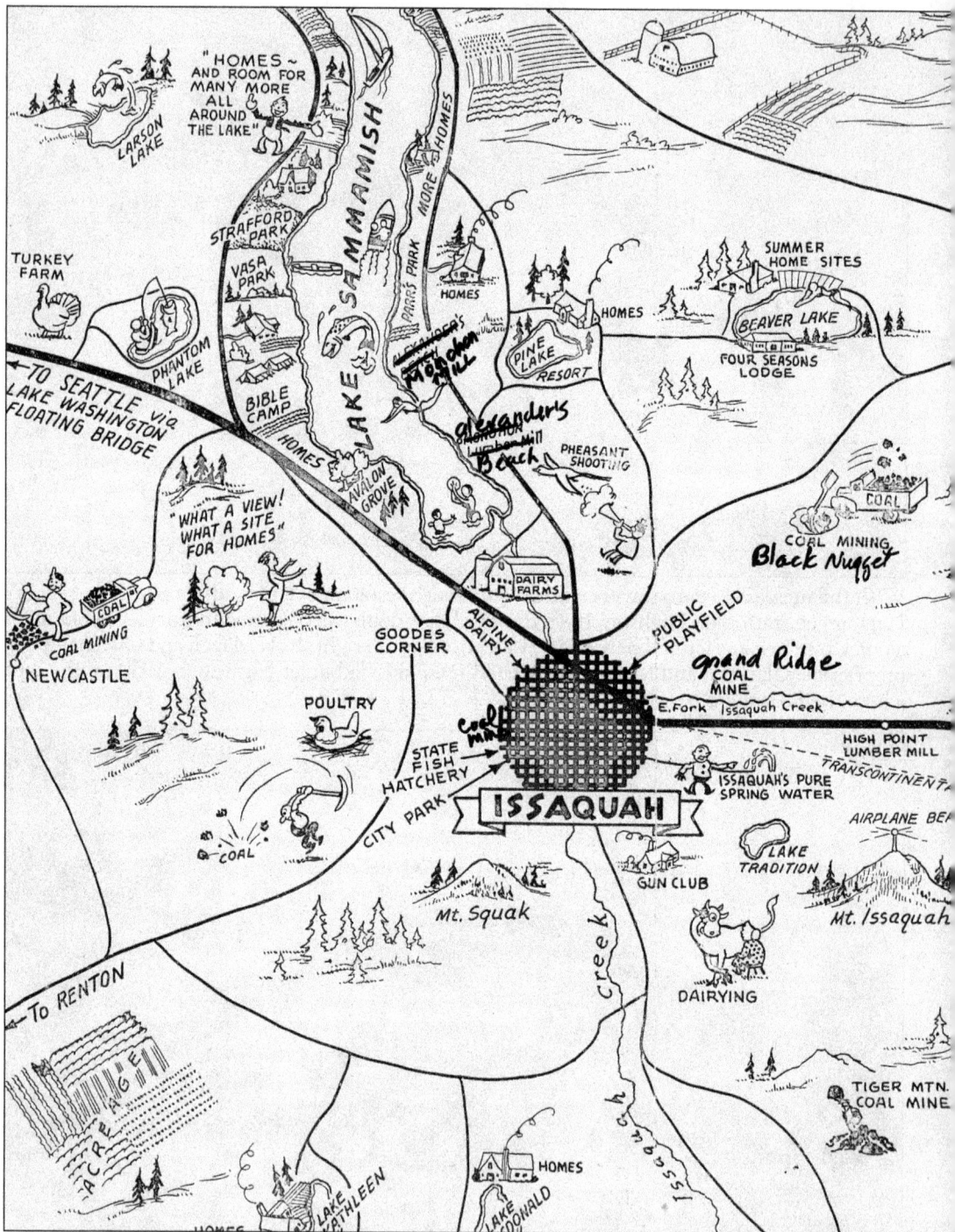

This map, *c.* 1948, touts the many attractions of the Issaquah Valley and environs. These include the sites important to historic industry, such as the lumber mills at High Point and Preston and coal mines at Newcastle and Grand Ridge, as well as recreation sites like the Mt. Si Golf Course and the Four Seasons Lodge. The map is clearly a marketing tool intended to sell the area to prospective homeowners. The text trumpets, "What a view! What a site for homes!"

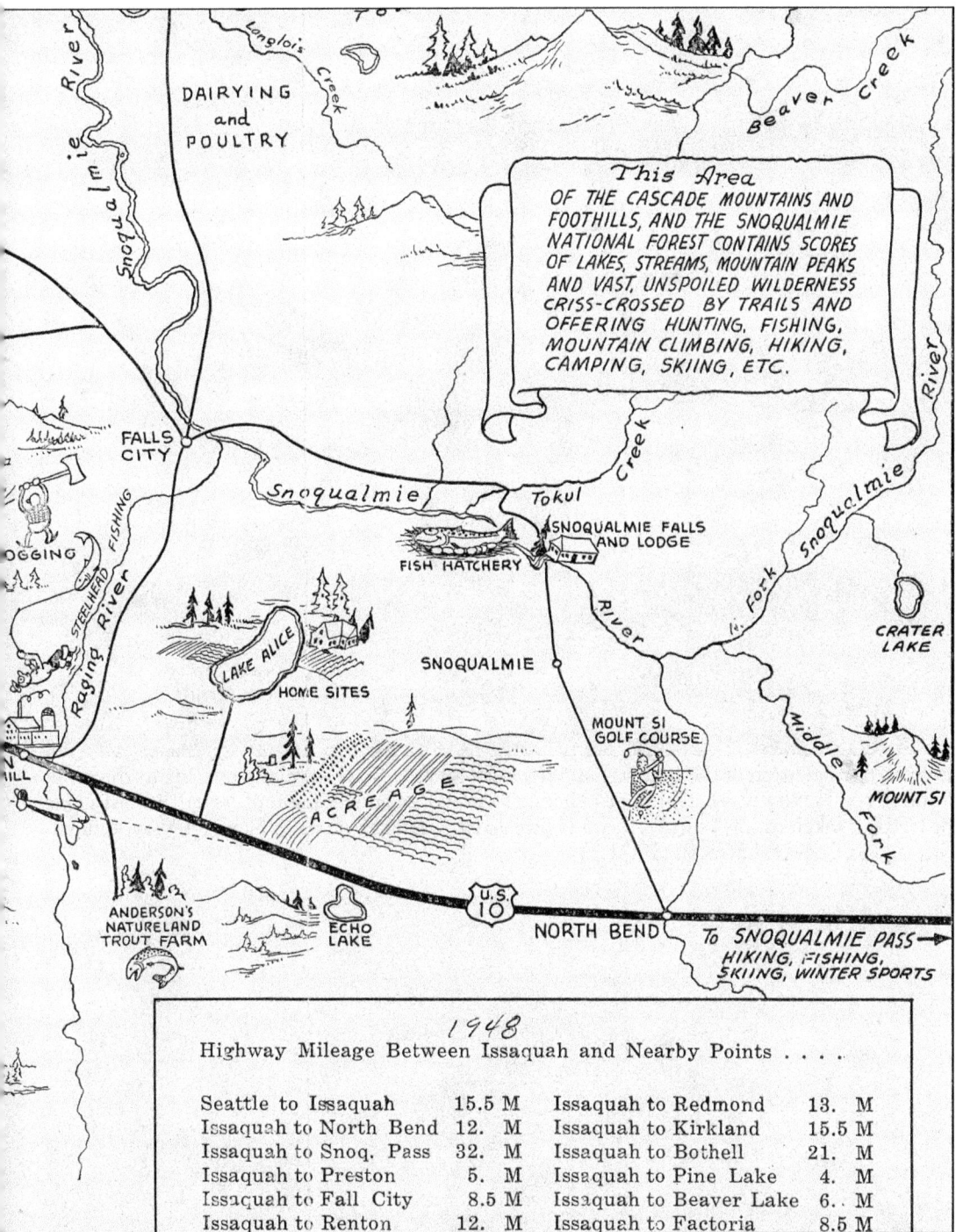

DAIRYING and POULTRY

Longlois Creek

Beaver Creek

Snoqualmie River

This Area
OF THE CASCADE MOUNTAINS AND FOOTHILLS, AND THE SNOQUALMIE NATIONAL FOREST CONTAINS SCORES OF LAKES, STREAMS, MOUNTAIN PEAKS AND VAST, UNSPOILED WILDERNESS CRISS-CROSSED BY TRAILS AND OFFERING HUNTING, FISHING, MOUNTAIN CLIMBING, HIKING, CAMPING, SKIING, ETC.

FALLS CITY

Snoqualmie

Tokul Creek

SNOQUALMIE FALLS AND LODGE

FISH HATCHERY

River

No. Fork Snoqualmie

LOGGING

STEELHEAD RIVER FISHING

Raging River

LAKE ALICE

HOME SITES

SNOQUALMIE

MOUNT SI GOLF COURSE

CRATER LAKE

Middle Fork

MOUNT SI

MILL

ACREAGE

U.S. 10

ANDERSON'S NATURELAND TROUT FARM

ECHO LAKE

NORTH BEND

To SNOQUALMIE PASS →
HIKING, FISHING, SKIING, WINTER SPORTS

1948
Highway Mileage Between Issaquah and Nearby Points . . . .

Seattle to Issaquah	15.5 M	Issaquah to Redmond	13. M
Issaquah to North Bend	12. M	Issaquah to Kirkland	15.5 M
Issaquah to Snoq. Pass	32. M	Issaquah to Bothell	21. M
Issaquah to Preston	5. M	Issaquah to Pine Lake	4. M
Issaquah to Fall City	8.5 M	Issaquah to Beaver Lake	6.. M
Issaquah to Renton	12. M	Issaquah to Factoria	8.5 M

and "Homes—and room for many more all around the lake." Chamber of Commerce literature from the same era also seems to offer everything the prospective homebuyer could ever want, right here in Issaquah. These pitches were wildly successful. Between 1940 and 1960, Issaquah's population increased from 812 to 1,870—an increase of more than 100 percent. By 1970, the town's population would reach 4,313.

Between the addition of the highway and the push for real estate development, life in the rural farming community was beginning to change forever. This photograph of Issaquah's last large fir tree was taken in 1944 on Art Reppe's property (bounded by today's Newport Way, Juniper Street, and Dogwood Street). (94.21.3)

Three

ENTERING AN
ERA OF CHANGE
1960–PRESENT

The population of Issaquah, stable from 1900 to 1950, began to grow in the 1950s. Between 1950 and 1970, Issaquah's population leaped from 955 to 4,313. Chamber of Commerce brochures from this era invited people to make their home in Issaquah, describing the town as located conveniently near Seattle and commercially viable, with small-town charm and friendly community members. Hallmarks of the small town began to disappear as houses, roads, and shopping centers filled the landscape. The new I-90 freeway contributed to the real estate boom and necessitated the removal of the Issaquah railroad trestle. The Issaquah Skyport also fell prey to commercial development.

Citizens reacted to these changes by working to preserve the distinguishing elements of the town they called home. In 1972 the Issaquah Historical Society formed, dedicating itself to the preservation of Issaquah's history. Innovative minds found a way to preserve many historic buildings in a shopping area known as Gilman Village. Citizen groups like Issaquah Residents for Environmental Quality formed and lobbied the city council on quality of life issues.

Today, Issaquah has grown into a thriving city with a population of roughly 13,000. Although growth and development changed the face of Issaquah, elements of its original character remain. Long-time resident Clint Brady wrote in *Preserving the Memories of Issaquah*, "I still feel like I'm coming home every time I crest the valley on I-90. . . . I sweep away the asphalt, buildings, and cars and let my mind wander back to the airport, cow fields, and farms. The real Issaquah is still there, it's just a little harder to see."

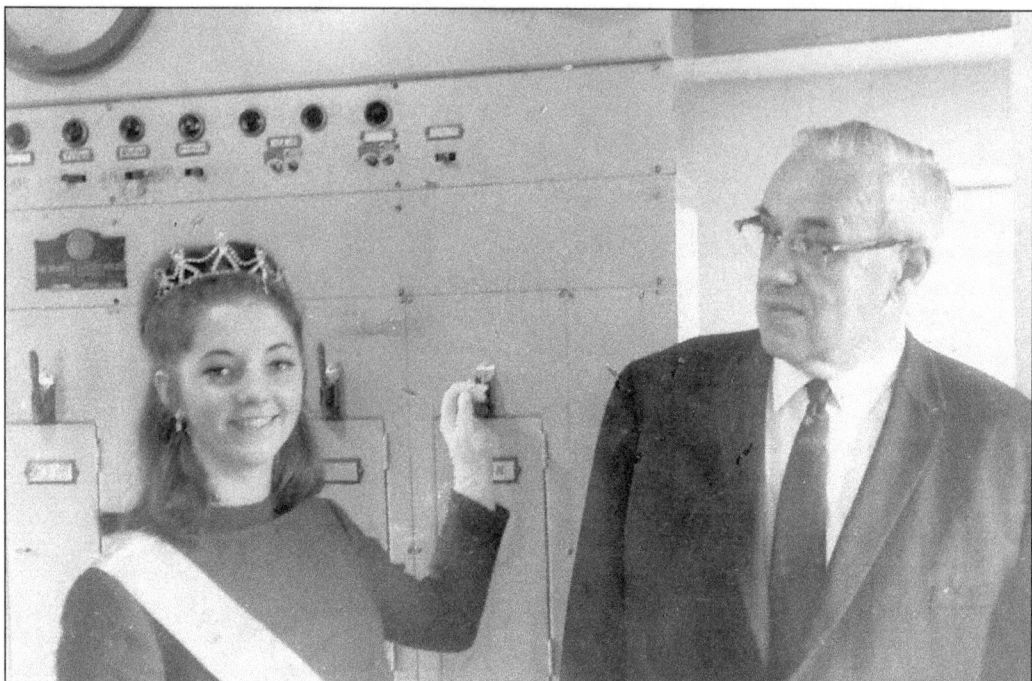

William Flintoft was Issaquah's mayor from 1956 until 1970. During his tenure the city's population quadrupled. In this 1968 photograph, Flintoft and Miss Issaquah (Colleen Dixon) preside at the opening of the new sewage treatment plant. No doubt Dixon and Flintoft were both called upon to fill more glamorous obligations in their respective positions. Later, Dixon became the second Miss Issaquah to compete in pageants at the national level. (72.21.14.97)

In December of 1960, City Ordinance 752 changed the names of 26 downtown streets. Mill Street became Sunset Way and Front Street was changed to Tenth Avenue. In 1970, Ordinance 939 further altered street names, and Tenth Avenue reverted to Front Street again. In this 1961 photograph, a new sign is installed on the corner of Tenth Avenue and Sunset Way. (72.21.14.187B)

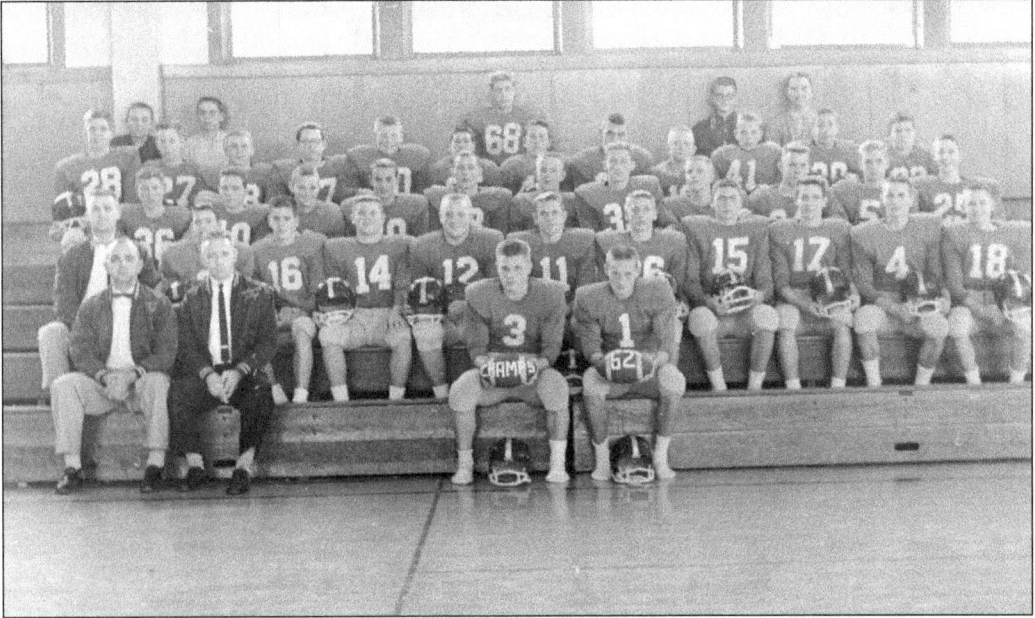

The 1962 Issaquah Junior High School football team poses on the gym bleachers. This team won the district's first junior high football championship in that year. (2001.30.4)

This high school was constructed in 1931, and was in use from 1932 until 1962. The newer building, in use from 1963 until 1990, withstood the 1965 earthquake with no damage. The junior high school, however, was damaged beyond repair by the same quake. (87.150.31)

J.R. Stephenson was Issaquah's postmaster from 1937 until 1966. In 1963, the post office was moved from the lower floor of the Masonic Hall (where this photograph was taken) into its own facility on Sunset Way. (72.21.14.281A)

Hans Jensen was a familiar figure in Issaquah. Jensen was remembered as a compassionate man with a soft spot for the town's youth. Jensen left his land to Issaquah's youngsters in his will. After his death in 1957, 65 acres were added to Lake Sammamish State Park to form a youth camping area. The area was dedicated in 1966. (88.15.3)

Bill Bergsma Sr. was well-known in Issaquah for his role as the town's perennial Santa Claus. Bergsma, a life-long Issaquah resident, passed away in 1997. Here, Santa rides down Front Street in a covered wagon. (93.20.6.3)

This candid photograph of 1966 Clark Elementary staff offers a glimpse of the camaraderie among some of Issaquah's best-known and much-loved residents at that time. Pictured, from left to right, are: (front row) Jean Jaekel, Luella Grant, Bob Eiene, Sue Smith, Polly Heft, Janie Link, Louise Quistorff, and Ron Reed; (middle row) Clella Menold, Emma Crow, Mary Boyden, Sylvia Bender, Pearl Deering, Agnes Hammond, Carol King, Joan Krivasha, and Bob Reed; (back row) Mary Whelus, Betty Evans, Ruth Colingham, Shirley Hayes, Marian Oules, Eleanor Hope, Margaret Medalon, Agnes Houdek, Mabel Miles, Cleo Somsak, Joe Zimmerman, and Ray Upton. (72.21.14.22H)

Janice Ott was one of two women abducted from Lake Sammamish State Park (pictured below in 1999) by Ted Bundy. Ott and Denise Naslund both disappeared from the park in separate incidents on July 14, 1974. Their remains were found together on Taylor Mountain about two months later. Before his execution in 1989, Ted Bundy confessed to their murders, along with the murders of 26 other women. (93.20.14, at left, and 2002.27.1, below)

Interstate 90 was constructed in the late 1960s and early 1970s. I-90 changed the face of Issaquah, as Highway 10 had before it. Getting to Seattle took even less time, and even more people were encouraged to move into the Issaquah area. June Day Sandberg reflects, "It wrecked our valley; changed our little town forever!" This photograph of I-90 was taken in 2001. (2002.27.2)

Generations of Issaquah residents experienced the railroad as a childhood backdrop. Mischievous memories of hopping a train to the beach or greasing the rails abound. Pictured, from left to right, are Kevin Horn, Gwynn Finney, Pammy McLoughlin, and Kurt Horn, who wave at a passing Burlington Northern freight train in 1967. (2000.21.3)

During the course of 1975 the Issaquah trestle was slowly dismantled to make way for an I-90 overpass. For many, the trestle was a symbol of Issaquah's identity as an active railroad town. (2001.21.1)

Rail service to the Darigold creamery continued until 1996, when the local branch line was finally vacated. Grass and other vegetation grows through the tracks in this August 2000 photograph. (2002.27.3)

The last Labor Day celebration was held in 1969. Harriet Fish cited volunteer fatigue as the cause of the festival's demise; others claim that revelry degenerated into outright rowdiness too often for the local authorities' liking. Labor Day celebrations were replaced by Salmon Days, in honor of the salmon returning to Issaquah Creek to spawn. This 1982 Salmon Days parade photograph shows Gilman Boulevard before construction of the many shopping centers and restaurants that line the street today. (2001.20.3)

The Salmon Days festival brings thousands of visitors to the town, and raises much needed revenue for the Issaquah Chamber of Commerce. In 1970, 2,500 people attended the first Salmon Days event. By 2000, the average attendance of this nationally known festival had grown to 250,000. In this 2000 photograph, throngs gather on and around the decking of the restored depot. (2002.27.4)

Like Labor Day and rodeo festivities before it, Salmon Days always features a parade down Front Street, as shown in this 2002 photograph. Many long-time residents are still wistful about the loss of the smaller, more intimate Labor Day festivities. In response to this need, the Chamber also sponsors a Down Home Fourth of July celebration, which caters to Issaquah residents. (2002.27.5)

The Labor Day Queen and Miss Issaquah have both been replaced by a royal couple, King and Queen Sammamish. In 2001, Lynn Rehn and Michael Johnson were Issaquah's elected royalty. The tradition of selecting royalty by ticket sales has also evolved: guests who buy tickets to Chamber of Commerce events may vote for their favorite candidates at that event. (2002.27.6)

The Issaquah Skyport began as a flight training facility during World War II. In 1961, Linn Emrich leased the Skyport and founded the Seattle Sky Sports Club, whose mission was to "encourage the use of the sky as a playground." The club offered training in gliding and ballooning also, but parachuting was the most popular option. (2001.17.17)

For a fee of $10, Seattle Sky Sports participants could learn the basics of parachuting at ground school. For $20, you could also make your first jump—but only if you were a man. Women were "invited to attend the ground school with husband or boyfriend free of charge." The Seattle Sky Sports Club also hosted air shows on a regular basis. Many fans would come week after week to watch the jumps and the other sky sports that took place there. (2001.35.3)

SEATTLE SKY SPORTS

PROGRAM

HOSTS THE...
PARACHUTE CLUB OF AMERICA
1963 NATIONAL
PARACHUTE
CHAMPIONSHIPS
AND
U.S. TEAM TRYOUTS
SEPT. 14-22 SEATTLE SKYPORT
ISSAQUAH
FREE ADMISSION & PARKING

50¢

113

For nearly 30 years, the Skyport provided recreation for jumpers and spectators of all ages. In this photograph, the Easter Bunny waves cheerfully while his parachute settles onto the field. (2001.17.15)

After the building boom began in the 1980s, the grassy field that Emrich leased for the Skyport became prime real estate for developers. In 1987 Emrich's lease expired, and a bond issue aimed at keeping the Skyport was defeated. Many long-time residents still remember the Skyport and mourn its loss. Today the field where mock dogfights were once held is the Pickering Place shopping center. (2001.17.14)

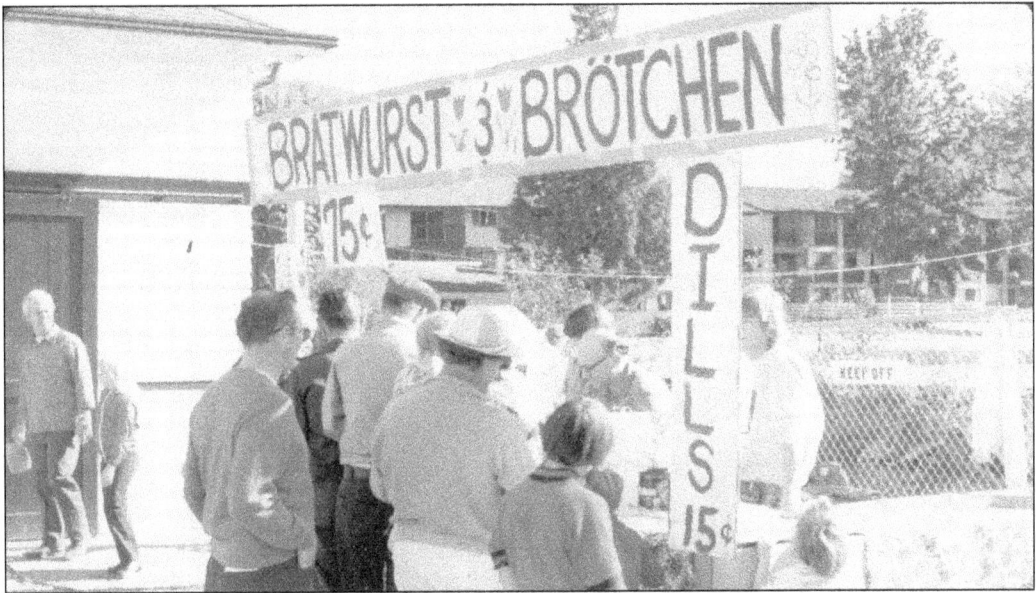

Rapid development encouraged concerned citizens to found Issaquah Residents for Environmental Quality (IREQ) in the 1970s. IREQ strove to improve the quality of life in a quickly growing Issaquah. One of their great victories was a reformed sign code that prevented billboards from marring the landscape. As a fundraiser, IREQ sold bratwurst and other snacks during Salmon Days. (2001.20.2)

The Gibson house, once the stately Victorian era home of former mayor W.E. Gibson, was razed in 1970. The loss of this and other historic buildings in Issaquah inspired residents to begin preserving the history that remained. In the mid-1960s, Edwards and Harriet Fish began recording Issaquah's history and photographing buildings and homes about to disappear. Harriet Fish played a critical role in founding the Issaquah Historical Society in 1972. (72.21.14.221B)

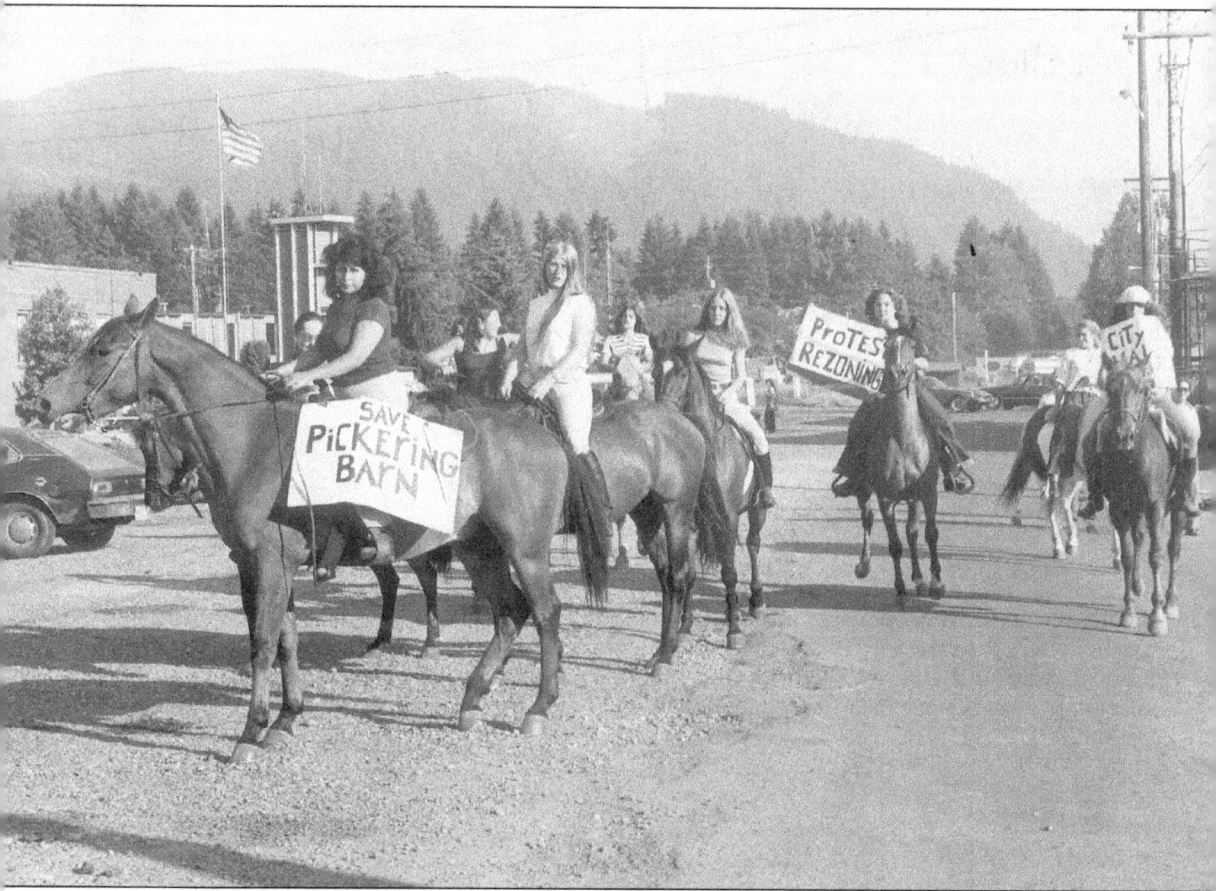

In this photograph, c. 1985, citizen activists protest a rezoning that would endanger the Pickering barn by opening the area to business development. In 1993, Langly Associates donated the barn to the City of Issaquah, which funded its restoration. Issaquah residents have been very involved in advocating the barn's preservation and restoration over the years. A committee of residents also worked closely with the city in determining the barn's eventual use. (93.20.6.6)

William Pickering Jr. constructed the Pickering barn, pictured above in 1999, in the 1890s. It was placed on the National Registry of Historic Places in 1983. Today the City of Issaquah Parks and Recreation Department operates the barn as a rental facility. It is also the location of the Issaquah Public Market, pictured below. (2002.27.7, above, and 2002.27.8, below)

In 1972, Betty Konarski convinced developers Marvin and Ruth Mohl that historic buildings slated for demolition could be moved and refurbished for use as a shopping center. Gilman Village was the result. Popular with visitors, Gilman Village (pictured in 1999) consists of more than 20 historic buildings, now used as shops. (2002.27.9)

In 1983 the Issaquah Historical Society encouraged the City of Issaquah to purchase the dilapidated Issaquah Depot. The depot had been closed up for nearly 30 years, and was in use as a ceiling tile warehouse at that time. (Courtesy of Greg Spranger)

The Historical Society pledged to take on the task of restoring the depot. The job was more extensive than anyone realized it would be, requiring more than a decade and significant donations of money and materials. Some parts of the depot had to be completely reconstructed. In this photograph, the roof has been torn out for replacement. (Courtesy of Greg Spranger)

Dedicated volunteers donated thousands of hours to the project. (Courtesy of Greg Spranger)

Today, the Issaquah Depot is on the National Registry of Historic Places. It houses one of the Issaquah Historical Society's two museums. It is also the Issaquah Valley Trolley's point of departure. (Courtesy of Barb Justice)

In this 2001 photograph, Mayor Ava Frisinger speaks at the inaugural run of the Issaquah Valley Trolley. Frisinger is Issaquah's second female mayor. She was elected in 1997, and re-elected in 2001. The Issaquah Valley Trolley, a project of the Issaquah Historical Society, aims to restore passenger rail service to Issaquah. (2002.27.10)

Various dignitaries attended the Issaquah Valley Trolley's inaugural run on April 30, 2001. These included King County Executive Ron Sims (left-hand seat, third from front), Issaquah's chief of police Dag Garrison (standing at back of car, in sunglasses), and Issaquah mayor Ava Frisinger (across the aisle from Sims). The trolley runs from the depot to the Issaquah Visitor's Center; in the future, the Issaquah Historical Society hopes the trolley will continue to points beyond. (2002.27.11)

In 2000 the City of Issaquah's new city hall and police station opened. The building was designed to complement the adjacent pedestrian walkway and Memorial Field. It also features a large rotunda for community use. (2002.27.12)

The Issaquah Salmon Hatchery hosts more than 300,000 visitors every year. In 1992 planning began for a series of remodels. By the time work was completed in 2002, improvements had been made to benefit salmon and human alike. New elements include the rearing ponds, the Watershed Science Center, interactive exhibits, and this handsome bronze sculpture of two salmon, named Gilda and Finley. (2002.27.13)

In 2001, the first Krispy Kreme donut store in the Pacific Northwest opened in Issaquah. The store generated sales of $452,000 in its first week, a Krispy Kreme record. Issaquah residents were surprised by the flood of donut fans who traveled from far and wide, and then stood in long lines in order to buy these treats. For a while it seemed that Issaquah and Krispy Kreme might become synonymous in the Pacific Northwest. By the time this photograph was taken in 2002, some of the furor had died down. (2002.27.14)

In spite of new growth in Issaquah, some elements of the small town remain. Among these is the last XXX Root Beer stand in America, pictured here in 1999. The XXX serves up 1950s style hamburgers and milkshakes, and often hosts vintage automobile shows. (2002.27.15)

Issaquah Creek, called Squak Creek by early settlers, flows through downtown Issaquah and into Lake Sammamish. Although threatened by development and environmental degradation, the creek continues to provide a habitat for Coho, Chinook, and Sockeye salmon. It also provides residents with glimpses of its natural beauty from various points throughout town. This photograph, taken in 1999, shows the portion of Issaquah Creek that flows past the Pickering barn. (2002.27.17)

Index

128

www.ingramcontent.com/pod-product-compliance
Lightning Source LLC
Chambersburg PA
CBHW050638110426
42813CB00007B/1848